*Other Books by Barbara Woodhouse*

NO BAD DOGS

WALKIES

BARBARA'S WORLD OF HORSES AND PONIES

# Just Barbara
## My Story

Barbara Woodhouse

SUMMIT BOOKS

NEW YORK

Copyright © 1986 by Barbara Woodhouse
All rights reserved
including the right of reproduction
in whole or in part in any form
Published by SUMMIT BOOKS
A Division of Simon & Schuster, Inc.
Simon & Schuster Building
1230 Avenue of the Americas
New York, New York 10020
SUMMIT BOOKS and colophon are trademarks of
Simon & Schuster, Inc.
Designed by Eve Kirch
Manufactured in the United States of America

10  9  8  7  6  5  4  3  2  1

Library of Congress Cataloging in Publication Data

Woodhouse, Barbara.
  Just Barbara.
    1. Woodhouse, Barbara.        2. Dog trainers—
England—Biography.     3. Horse trainers—
England—Biography. I Title.
SF422.82.W66A3   1986      636.08'8'0924 [B]      86-14470

ISBN: 0-671-46248-2

# Acknowledgments

The author and publishers are grateful to the following for permission to reproduce the photographs indicated:

The BBC for photograph 57; the *Daily Express* for photograph 62; the *Daily Mirror* for photograph 38; Home Counties Newspapers Ltd for photograph 59; Keystone press for photographs 35, 47, and 48; Paramount Press for photograph 37; Pictorial Press Ltd for photograph 34; Reveille for photograph 54; the *Sun* for photographs 41, 44, and 63; Syndication International for photograph 60.

# Contents

# Just Barbara

# Early Days

The first thing I remember clearly is the birth of my baby sister, Hazel, when I was eighteen months old. A maternity nurse of ample proportions took over our nursery. She wore a navy blue dress and a long starched apron which, owing to its prickly stiffness, would have effectively kept one from hugging her even if one had wanted to. What fascinated me most about her were her rosy cheeks surmounted by a frilly white bonnet cap tied under her chin. I clearly remember her bringing "your new baby sister" down the stairs leading to our nursery and sitting before the roaring log fire with a bundle so wrapped in starched white garments and a huge woollen shawl that, at first, I saw no sister at all. On peeping closer I saw a mass of straight black hair surrounding a tiny little face; she was fast asleep. I tried to touch her but was gently pushed back by Nurse Kite and told just to look. This seemed to me to be an awfully dull thing to do with a new sister, so I went off to play with Nanny and my other sister, Nadine (Dene for short), who was eighteen months older than me. We both had dolls and lots of toy animals. Dene had a lovely doll with big eyes, real hair and lots of clothes, all of which could be taken off, washed and put back. I had a rather inferior doll which I called Vera after my aunt, but my favourite toy was Beeky Bar, a duck made of lots of coloured pieces of felt with boot buttons as eyes. Even at this early age I preferred animals, and it was lucky for us, especially for me, that Nanny was also an animal lover, for our nursery always housed some sick animal, a bird with a broken wing or a rabbit with a chill.

I soon lost interest in my new sister as she did not want to play and she made horrible screaming noises. I do not know why but it remains very clearly in my mind that at that particular time I was in the way; everyone seemed busy fussing over the new sister. My mother lay in bed with her golden hair spread all over the pillow, and she did not get up for our playtime, which was normally at five o'clock, after tea, when we were dressed in our very best party clothes and taken down to the drawing room for an hour. Now we did not do this; we stayed upstairs in the nursery or went and sat on Mummy's bed while she read to us, but I could not sit still for long and went back to Nanny in the nursery, who was always willing to play and did not seem to pay much attention to the new baby sister. I am sure that it was this memory of a new baby being a hindrance to my normal existence which made me hate babies in my early days.

The nursery wing at St Columba's College, Rathfarnham, County Dublin, the boys' public school where my father was headmaster, was at the top of the very large headmaster's house. An enormously wide flight of stone steps led to it. Halfway up was a large window looking out onto the beautiful flower border and lawns of which my mother was so fond. A large breeding cage for Nanny's canaries and a smaller cage for my sister's budgerigars hung from this window. Besides talking, Dene had taught her two budgerigars innumerable tricks, such as picking a card from a pack of fortune-telling cards. The birds were tame and used to fly about in our nursery but although they were very lovable, I was far more interested in animals.

The first nine years of my life were spent at St Columba's with my two sisters and brother. We were brought up in this glorious place with one hundred and fifty acres of woods and moorland behind us and a long-distance view of the sea. We had two dogs, a large rough Collie called Sandy and a little black Pomeranian called Jim, both of whom lived in the nursery. Jim followed us everywhere but Sandy was too big to come with us on the daily afternoon pony trap outings Mother considered essential for our health. It did not matter what the weather was like, we still had to go out. In freezing weather, Jim would lie on the floor under the large waterproof rug lined with navy blue wool which covered us all up, and he would keep our feet warm. Nanny always drove the pony although after my fourth birthday she would let me take the reins. I loved the pony and, much to the displeasure of the groom, was forever feeding it sugar, even when it was waiting at the front door to take us all on our drive. In those days the bits were made of steel and took a lot of burnishing, which was made harder by the sugary mess left on the bit.

Our ponies were always being changed. They came from the local horse dealer on a week's trial. If we did not like the pony or it had some vice like shying, he would bring another, always just that much more expensive, until in the end my father was paying an exorbitant price to get the right pony. However, we finally did get a lovely little bay pony, and when I was five I drove it myself each day to Dundrum to fetch our governess. Once we met an enormous steamroller resurfacing the road and the pony would not go past this monster. One of the road workers had to lead the pony along the road, but once past it went like the wind. The pony and I had a great rapport and the faster it went, the happier I was. My governess was not so sure she liked this and was always asking me to slow down, but I paid no attention.

This pony was only for the trap. The whole family was taught to ride at a very early age on Pamela, Mother's black donkey whom she had had as a girl and who was very old. When I was two, I was put on her in a sort of saddle basket to which I was strapped and led about. It was not long before I was telling Nanny to let go, I wanted to ride alone. Pamela seemed to sense my happiness for she was quite willing to go where I wanted, which was up and down the drive leading to our house. Later on, I had a grey donkey of my own who had a baby donkey. We called them Bluebell and Violet and when I was about six, I broke in Violet, who was then about eighteen months old. I got on her first by climbing on a box at the side while Hazel held her on a halter. We had no saddle to fit such a tiny donkey. Then it was Hazel's turn to climb up, and I ran up and down with her. Hazel was three years old then. She and I were the only members of the family to really enjoy riding. Charlie, my elder brother, loathed it, but in those days in Ireland everyone rode as a matter of course, and he had to learn like the rest of us. He was terrified of cantering and fell off several times despite the fact that we had a lovely quiet bay pony. I think the pony probably sensed his nerves.

During the Irish rebellion of 1916, we were out one afternoon in the pony trap when the groom came rushing up on one of the work horses and told Nanny to drive back to the college as quickly as she could. He had heard that we were on the list of those to be murdered by the Sinn Feiners because we were English. On our return to the college, we learned that there had been a raid on the armoury where the guns the boys used in the army training school corps were stored and all of them had been stolen. That evening we watched the main post office in Dublin burn down through my father's telescope on the roof of the college. We thought it very exciting!

Every morning, we had lessons in a big study where the walls were covered with ancient tapestries of great value, and there was an old piano in one corner. I remember how bored I was having painstakingly to write beautiful script. I am sure this is why my writing is so bad today. When we had to go to another school I had to learn to write all over again, this time joining up the letters!

Our governesses came and left with such regularity that it was difficult to keep up with them. We were five high-spirited children and were always up to tricks. I say five because Charlie, my elder brother, was rather shy and Mother and Father thought he should have a companion of his own age to bring him out, so Willie Telford, a relative of the famous organ makers, was brought into our family circle. He was an outgoing boy, redheaded and freckled, full of fun and quite lovely to live with. He and Charlie became great friends. One day, I remember Charlie and Willie climbing onto the roof of the boot shed where the school boot boy cleaned all the boys' boots. The governess, who was then a Miss Pattison, had to pass by this shed on leaving the pony trap to get to our schoolroom; she was a prim lady in whose eyes we could do nothing right, so we were always up to pranks. This time she got more than she expected as Charlie and Willie had hauled the garden hose up onto the roof, pretending to wash it down, and completely soaked her when she passed underneath. Despite their abject apologies, Miss Pattison left on the spot.

The next governess was a gentle Miss Wand, whom we all liked, and at last our education progressed. In fact she was the one who suggested the boys build a hut in the park adjoining the school so that in hot weather we could have our lessons there. This really endeared her to us all, and when the hut was finished and the crevices filled with moss, we used to go there for our lessons, right up to the end of September, if the weather was fine.

One of the things that fascinated me about Miss Wand was the succulent way she had of eating her elevenses, which was brought to her on a dainty tray by one of the school maids. This always consisted of two thin heavily buttered slices of white bread, a tiny china pot of tea, milk and sugar. When she ate the bread, her lips became moist, which made the thin slices of bread and butter seem all the more tasty. I always felt hungry just watching her and wondered why we never got elevenses. I for one, however, did not need them because I loved food and would have gotten far too fat (not that the school food was appetizing, just filling). The school food sent up from the kitchen to the nursery in a lift was typical of boys' meals in those days: figs, bread and butter pudding, etc. Nanny was very strict with us, never allowing us to get down from table until we had left a clean plate. I have sat from lunch until tea time in front of a plate of baked custard and figs or prunes knowing that I would be sick if I ate either one of them. I tried hiding the figs under the handles of my spoon and fork but Nanny always found me out. If I remember rightly I was eventually allowed to leave the uneatable offering by tea time.

I was Nanny's favourite in spite of the fact that I was the naughtiest of the family. One day, as a punishment for some naughtiness, she put me in the corner by a large curtain which hung from the window. Her knitting bag was dangling on a hook behind the curtain and by the time I was allowed out of the corner, I had unravelled a large piece of knitting. I got a smacking for this, but we were rarely punished in this way as Nanny loved us dearly. She must have worked like a slave to have looked after the five of us as well as making all our clothes. She only had one day off a month and was paid forty pounds a year. In those days babies were fed twice in the night; how she managed, I don't know. Her first position had been with Sir Henry Wood looking after his children. When they no longer needed a nanny she came to us, where she stayed until we were grown up.

We really loved Nanny more than our mother or father at that time because our parents were distant, slightly terrifying people whom we only saw after tea for an hour when we went down to the drawing room. There my mother played endless games like ludo and halma with us. (The first, a form of pachesi played in the British isles; the second, a game for two to four players where each player attempts to move his or her pieces from the home corner to a corresponding position on the opposite side of the board.) Or she read books to us. Everything was for our enjoyment, yet somehow with me it failed. I remember the card games when, at an early age, I realized that if I cheated, my mother would get extremely angry and send me out of the drawing room back upstairs to Nanny. This was exactly what I wanted. The lectures on how I should end up in hellfire if I cheated had little effect, although every Sunday after tea the Bible was read to us by my father, who was a clergyman as well as headmaster. He always chose rather lurid passages from the Bible which should have put the fear of cheating or any other sin firmly into our minds, but as the Bible also says our sins would be forgiven, I could not see why we were supposed to be so frightened of burning in hell. Even today, I fail utterly to understand religion. I cannot see how God can possibly sort us out when we get to the gates of heaven or hell. Surely the sins we commit every day of our lives, like saying unkind things, or envying those with more possessions than we have, cannot be easily judged against those of, say, child murderers. Now I prefer not to think about it. I have a code which I have set myself of trying to say sorry every night before the sun goes down to those I have hurt. I try to help those who need my help, but beyond that, I claim nothing. I do not go to church because I can pray better in the fields. I wrote a hymn called "By Your Side" which has been published and just about sums up my view on religion, which is that however much life hurts you, God is there to help you if you need Him. I do not believe prayers always get answered; I shall never comprehend why God allows such terrible things to happen to one in this life if He is all-loving, yet perhaps it is for His profit and loss account and I trust and believe in Him. Three times in my life I have nearly died, and each time I felt at complete peace with no fear at all. This must be of comfort to anyone fearing death.

Early childhood memories were always those of getting on the right side of people. I was a very happy child, and I loved all people; no one was my enemy. This faith in people led me into all sorts of queer situations; there was the old thief of a butler in our household who stole biscuits and whisky, and when I was about eight, he invited me into his pantry to taste a nip of the "strong stuff." It nearly choked me and from that day I have never liked drink. In fact even one glass of champagne goes straight to my head and makes me giddy, so if I am at a wedding, I seldom take more than a tiny sip and then palm it off onto my husband.

After my father died, and I was only nine at the time, I always acted as intermediary between my mother and irritable tradespeople. Mother came from a long line of ancestors who in the old days would have been called the ruling classes. Her crest was an arm and a hand holding a whip, and her maiden name was Masterman. I often wonder whether the family had originally been horse trainers or dog trainers—or were we slave traders? Mother never seemed to think that regulations were made for her and her terrific charm usually surmounted all obstacles, but occasionally a little inside help smoothed her path. I think she never accepted the word "can't" and I have inherited this; defeat is something I have never learned to accept. Unfortunately one cannot always win, and most of my sleepless nights, of which I have many, are spent trying to solve the insoluble.

Bed to me has always seemed purgatory because at the age of sixteen I seriously injured my back playing hockey and slipped a disc. That is why for the whole of my life, except to have children, I have never spent one single day in bed through illness. If I am ill, which has only happened twice in forty years, being a speed reader I can read as many as three books a day sitting by the fire. I have the odd feeling that if I have flu the best thing to do is to wrap up, get out into the cold and not give the germs the comfort of hot drinks, hot-water bottles and warmth. They soon find a more comfortable body to invade! Because all my life I have had animals which do not understand that walks in the woods with a high temperature are not perhaps what the doctor ordered, and because cows cannot remain unmilked, I have built up this "mind over matter" resistance to illness.

I often wonder how much is mapped out years and years ahead, and think of the funny coincidences that happen. I well remember our early days at the Irish school where the first years of our lives were spent, the happy carefree years in an atmosphere of rigid discipline, lots of joyful entertainment and education in its widest sense. We were taught to dance, to play the piano, to act, to speak correctly. We had painting lessons every Wednesday with Miss Yeats, W. B. Yeats's sister. We would spend two hours painting, mostly flowers in pots, or hawthorn on brown paper, which looked very nice if you had an aptitude for this sort of painting. Hazel and Dene did, and eventually Hazel became a very good artist, Dene preferring watercolour sketches. I did not shine at all and was considered quite unteachable. I was not even corrected for my appalling paintings, and it was a complete waste of Miss Yeats's time. Charlie did not want to paint in watercolours in spite of the fact that he showed great artistic promise, and as he wished to draw in pastels or crayons, William Orpen, later Sir William Orpen, came to the school once a week to give him lessons. Sir William Orpen was an Irish-born British portrait painter who lived from 1878 to 1931. At one time we had innumerable sketches by this famous artist lying about. He once brought the British painter and etcher Augustus John up to the school for the day and he did a beautiful sketch of Charlie which for years lay in the loft of our house at Oxford. What it would be worth today I do not know but I think it got thrown away when the loft was cleared.

Ballet was also part of my sisters' and my education. Every Saturday we were taken to a dancing school in

Dublin and fitted out with ballet shoes. We were expected to be graceful on the tips of our toes and to move our legs in a way I am sure nature never intended me to move mine. My toes just bent backwards and nearly touched my heels every time I stood on my points. The mistress gave me up after about six lessons and told Mother she was wasting her money. Dene and Hazel carried on and Hazel eventually became a lovely ballet dancer on the stage.

Etiquette and behaviour at home and in public formed a big part of our education. Every Sunday, Mother and Father would invite about twelve boys to tea in the drawing room. There would be four boys to each small table and Dene, Hazel and I would act as hostesses. We were taught to "keep the ball rolling," never to allow the conversation to lapse into awkward, lengthy pauses, and Mother would come around to each table to see how we were getting on. She had been brought up in St Petersburg where my grandfather had been an English banker and, in those days, an understanding of protocol and good behaviour was a requisite in high society. Mother taught us to encourage the boys to talk about themselves, about their interests, and not to monopolize the conversation ourselves. Above all, we were taught to see that no one, however drab, was left out of the party. This early training has left me with a basic security in public that has served me well. It made sure that we never thought of our own feelings in public and forgot our own shortcomings when talking to people, as it was the other person who mattered. It gave us a friendly out-look because we had been told that, however forbid-ding the exterior, there is always something worth finding in everyone.

Once a week, we were taught ballroom dancing. We learned the polka, the waltz, the hornpipe and the schottische. Again, the younger members of the school partnered us, arriving in their best suits, their hair slicked down with dreadful hair oil. It was my misfor-tune one afternoon to partner one young boy who had come dressed in a brown velvet suit which had the horrible smell that corduroy used to carry, and his hair was covered in coconut oil. However, in spite of these small irritations, we certainly learned to dance, and in later years Hazel and I taught ballroom dancing our-selves. Michael Foot and his brother, Dingle, were two of our pupils.

Some years later, when we moved to Oxford and the Christmas parties became numerous, these dancing les-sons were a great help. In those days, at parties, one had little program cards with a tiny pencil attached by a coloured cord with a fluffy piece on the end. No one was left a wallflower because the hostess made sure that she introduced as many young men to as many girls as were necessary to fill the girls' and boys' pro-gram cards. The young men fetched the girls from their chaperones and returned them to their seats after the dance. It was not good manners to book too many dances with the same girl as that would mean the plainer, less interesting girls would not have their cards filled in.

As we grew up, Mother would occasionally come and have a meal with us in the nursery and would critically watch our table manners. "Do not make such a noise when you are eating, eat more slowly, take your elbows off the table, do not drink with food in your mouth; if you have to speak with food in your mouth, be sure to push it into your cheek and do not open your mouth too wide . . ."

During the First World War our home in Ireland became a hive of activity. Mother trained as a Red Cross nurse, and her sister Vera, wife of Stanley Tomkins, the former Governor of Uganda who had volunteered again for service, came over from England to live with us. The drawing room became the room where all the action took place, such as rolling bandages and teaching first aid to young recruits of the Red Cross.

My mother started breeding Belgian hares for food and became the editor of the *Rabbit Keepers' Journal.* She wrote endless articles on how to keep rabbits for food and we all, however young, helped put the wrappers around the monthly magazine that went out to thousands of subscribers.

During the war, the Canadian army horses, their officers and grooms who had been billetted on us provided the greatest excitement for me. Among the officers was Mother's brother, Michael Masterman, who ran a ranch in Canada and adored horses. He loved my obvious enjoyment of them and carried me on the front of the saddle of his charger whenever he had time to spare. I was always to be found in the park among the legs of these great horses, whenever I managed to escape from Nanny's watchful eye. The gentle way they took sugar or carrots from me, with their lips almost kissing my fingers, made it quite clear that they would not hurt me. Eventually, the officers and their horses were all sent overseas on active service. Sadly, Uncle Michael was killed within weeks of being sent out, which upset my mother terribly. She built a library at St Columba's in his memory and called it the Masterman Library.

Holidays every summer were great fun when we were young. A month used to be booked in a hotel by the sea and we would go to places like Bundoran. The entourage was quite large. My father had a Cadillac, my mother a Model T Ford. The whole family went, including Willie of course, the nursery maid, Nanny, and Jim, the Pomeranian. We could not take Sandy as he was too big. Father drove the Cadillac, the chauffeur Mother's Model T Ford.

There was a sort of pecking order as far as luggage was concerned. Mother and Father had huge brown trunks with a thick leather strap around them. As children, we had two trunks filled with every possible garment: combinations with long legs, woollen bands to go around our tummies, bathing suits made of alpaca which tied below the knees and up around the neck, and bathing caps which looked like pudding bowls made of green transparent waterproof material with elastic in them under which we stuffed our hair. It always amazed me that we were practically never uncovered on the beach, except for the brief period at sea. Our frilly dresses and hats were inevitably worn on the sojourns on the beach. In those days when one went bathing one did it from a bathing box drawn down to the sea edge. Mother taught us to wet our foreheads before dipping in to the sea, but what this was supposed to do, I don't know. We never plunged in as we would today, but held the skirt of our bathing suit and bobbed up and down. Eventually, with tremendous bravado, we dipped right up to our necks. Mother or Father held us under the chin with one hand, grabbed a large piece of bathing suit between our shoulders and taught us to swim by slowly loosening the hold on our suits. I took to swimming like a duck takes to water. The sea held no fear for me. In fact when I was four I remember once it was very rough, a huge wave was coming at us and, in his hurry to get out of the sea, Charlie gave me a shove to start himself off. The wave knocked me down and Nanny had to rush into the sea, fully clothed, to pull me out. She then had to be taken back to the hotel to change her soaking clothes. I was not at all frightened by the adventure.

I will never forget one August when we came to England for our holiday and went to the Lake District. Mother's Model T Ford would not go up the steep gradients and she had to back it up one hill as the reverse gear gave more power than the forward one! She never had another car after the Ford as she could not face the newfangled gearboxes. Motoring in those days was quite an adventure, especially in the first car we had. It took a considerable time, for example, to get the hood up if it rained. Any undue exertion on the car's part up a steep hill made the engine boil. The sharp flint roads were forever puncturing the tires. The dust made it necessary to wear hats with veils which completely covered our faces, and we had to shake our coats like dogs to get rid of our dust. We were covered up with enormous blue-lined fur rugs and the perennial picnic basket was full of hot refreshments and a thermos for the times we were sitting by the side of the road while the necessary repairs were done to the car. I do not remember a journey without these incidents. That was all part of the fun of holidays.

We were never without food of some sort and Nanny's canvas bag, which she seldom seemed to be without, always contained large packets of biscuits. We had waterproof knickers which we put on for paddling, in bright yellow waterproof material which pricked, plus all the buckets, the spades, the bathing suits, bathing caps and towels. I think Nanny and the nurserymaid were treated more like beasts of burden than like people. My greatest joy were the donkey rides on the beach. I was always to be found with the donkeys, even though we could not afford all the rides I would have wished for.

We only went away once a year, in August. Easter holidays were very much a religious celebration. Nanny made us all new outfits and I remember one in particular when we three girls had scarlet coats with black imitation fur collars and cuffs and bonnets to match and we went to the morning church service very proud of our new outfits. We usually spent the rest of the day at Easter time looking for wild violets and primroses.

Christmas was a tremendous celebration with an enormous Christmas tree in the school front hall and we drew and painted all our own Christmas cards. I cannot feel that the recipients of my efforts were very thrilled with them!

# Schooldays

After the era of governesses, Charlie and Willie joined the boys in the school where my father taught, for their lessons, and eventually, Dene and I joined them too. I do not talk much about my father as I knew him so little. To me he was a tall, rather fierce man with a moustache which pricked if he kissed me, someone who whacked my brother with a cane when he refused to take off his cap to a woman friend of my mother's whom we all loathed, someone who removed me quickly and firmly from the classroom when I was innocently passing a crib from the boy next to me to the one on my other side. I was the victim caught holding the crib when my father saw me, and the disgrace of being frog-marched from the classroom will remain with me forever. I do not know what happened to the boys; a beating I expect, for the cane was not spared at St Columba's in those days.

I wonder how much influence most fathers have on their daughters. Mine made me think that men were creatures to be well respected. My first love affair occurred when I was six. A party was being given on the headmaster's tennis lawn for twenty of the older boys to celebrate my father's birthday; strawberries and cream were the great treat. I sat next to a very handsome fair-haired boy with whom I fell in love at first sight. As a mark of my admiration, I gave him my strawberries, which he received with cool gratitude, but his interest in me went no further than that. For years I loved this handsome boy in a girlish dreamlike way. His name was Dermot Boyle. Then forty years later, a Lady Boyle rang me about the training of her poodle. We got talking about Ireland and when she discovered I was the daughter of the late headmaster of St Columba's College, she said her husband had been to school there. She was the wife of my first love! However, it was not until many years later when I attended the prize giving at my son's school, that there to give away the prizes was Air Vice Marshall Sir Dermot Boyle, the schoolboy I had fallen in love with when I was six. I still think that I had very good taste for one so young!

I am always referring to what my parents told me in my young days. Perhaps I am strange in this present-day world of despised parents to have modelled my life so much on what I was taught, but I firmly believe that experience is one of the most important things in life, and that anything my parents told me was right because they had had experience. This brings me to the fact that my father always insisted that we must never run up bills. If you wanted something you had to have the money to pay for it, or it was dishonest. What modern people would think of this advice I do not know, with all their credit systems and hire purchase; but it has always given me an inner peace to know that, with the exception of the telephone bill, I owe nobody anything. I utterly refuse to run up accounts. If I did, it would make the balance in my current account look bigger than it should be, and that gives one a false sense of well-being, stunts one's enterprise, and according to my father, makes one dishonest by living off other people's money. It is now obvious to me that one cannot make money with nothing behind one. All businesses are built up on credit, yet my conscience still says "You cannot buy what you have not got the money to pay for." Heaven knows which is right!

In my childhood days we were given only one penny a week. If we needed more than one penny a week, we could go to Mother and ask if there was any job to do whereby we could earn some money. She never refused to find us something to do, but it was not something easy. It made us realize the value of money; that extra one penny had to be gained by real effort or we did not get it. Ordinary things like cleaning the house or silver were part and parcel of our normal existence, and only the boys in the family escaped it. This I never understood. Mother even cleaned my younger brother's shoes for him. Many was the time that I remonstrated with her and suggested he be made to do this menial task for himself, but men in my mother's mind were creatures to be waited on hand and foot by their womenfolk. My elder brother did not agree, and he certainly did his share of heavier household tasks when we lived at Oxford after my father had died and our fleet of servants were things of the past. In my own household these things do not occur. I see nothing menial or unsuitable for men in the job of washing up, or even making beds.

My father had been a double blue in cricket and football at Oxford and played these games with the boys at St Columba's. One night, when I was nine years old, he died of a heart attack, although he had been playing football that afternoon, and Mother was left a widow with four children and another on the way. Willie had to return to his parents in Dublin and, with little sympathy from the school authorities, we had to leave Ireland as the house was required for another headmaster. Father had owned a house called Sandfield at Headington, four miles from Oxford, but at that time it was occupied by the Rowells, who owned a jewellery store in Oxford, and they had to be given a year's notice to leave, so we went to Brighton for a year, to a dull house in a row with no place for animals. It was a dreary, uneventful year so I will pass over it.

My brother Desmond was born in Brighton and Mother seemed completely smitten with him and used to say he was all she had left of Father. This, in my opinion, spoiled Desmond, or Bobby, as we called him after the title of a favourite book about a very naughty boy. Bobby was rather fat and he looked like the boy on the cover of that book. It was at that time, when I was about thirteen years old, that I wrote a long and illiterate poem on my hatred of babies. Bobby was a terrible screamer and at nights he kept us awake crying. All the baby foods in the world did not seem to suit him, so one night I asked if he could sleep in my room with his cot next to my bed, and when he cried, I used to pat him and say "thunder" in a very loud voice. This had the required effect; Bobby slept. Recently, I saw a television program which said the best thing to make children go to sleep was noise, so perhaps I was ahead of my time.

Bobby had seemingly non-caring nurserymaids, for throughout his early toddling days they all, with one exception, let him fall down the stairs. I cannot think how many times Bobby fell down the stairs without seriously hurting himself. The "bump, bump" we heard so often, will always remain in my memory. Why no one put a gate at the top I cannot think, or if they did, why was it not kept shut? One day I had to take him out with me on the bus to Oxford. His face was all bruises, and the terrible remarks from the other passengers made me feel very miserable. It all added up to the fact that I hated babies. Yet in years to come when I had my own, I doubt if any mother could have loved them more. Even though I had a nanny, ninety percent of the seeing after them was done by myself, which made the nannies feel useless and they left one by one. In the end, my own old nanny returned to me and took over and was not jealous of my wanting to care for my own children. Nanny lived to the age of ninety-eight, so it is obvious that hard work pays if you want to live a long life!

My change of heart towards children shows that one should never make up one's mind without leaving a loophole to alter one's opinion. The thing that always amazed me was that other people's children, when I was a youngster, did not recognize the fact that I was not overly keen on playing with them, and that I much preferred animals or sports of some kind. If I lay on the beach during our annual summer holiday in Cornwall, before long I would be surrounded by children. Sticky hands would go into mine, requests of "please play with us" would drag me to my feet, and before I knew where I was, I, the "baby hater," would be the play mother to dozens of kids. Is it that the human child has little or no telepathy, that its trusting mind sees someone who may look fun, and in its own conceit decides to make that person like it willy-nilly? I believe that to be true, or maybe it was that they knew the real me, who when I became grown-up, loved my children almost too much and certainly love other people's children too. I even taught for a short time in a kindergarten and I really enjoyed making up fairy stories to tell to wide-eyed youngsters, who believed every word, because I think I used an exciting tone of voice when recounting the made-up spontaneous tales.

Today, I have no youngsters to tell fairy tales to, but I use the same tone of voice with dogs who believe that this voice means exciting hunts in the woods, or work in a film, or just lovely "din dins." Without my early experiences with small children, I would never have realized what tone of voice can do to bring out the best, or even the worst, in both the animal and human kingdom. To this day, if I work in a film with a child, I can get it to do things quite happily that the director or its mother have been unable to get it to do. When my daughter Judith had her little girl, Harriet, she was ill after the birth and I took the baby home for a month. I was in my element and sent her back to her mother healthy and I hope, happy. I certainly felt like a mother again, rather than a grandmother.

Our holidays, when we were teenagers, were always great fun. Although we were desperately poor—Mother had only been left three hundred pounds a year to keep the house and family together—she always managed to save enough to take us to the sea, as of old, for the month of August, and we usually took two or three other children from friends' families with us so that if we went to dances or anything, we had the right number of boys and girls. Everyone in our family played musical instruments. I played the piano and Hawaiian guitar, Charlie played the banjo, Dene the mandoline, Mother the Spanish guitar and Bobby the percussion instruments so we had lovely singsongs after our days by the sea and our excursions. Our dogs, Andy the Alsatian and Vanity the fox terrier, always came with us. We usually had a charming landlady in the house we rented so holidays were very enjoyable.

We always went to all the regattas that took place in Cornwall in those days. As I was by that time a first-rate swimmer and fairly good at diving, I entered all the races and won quite a nice lot of pocket money. I remember once during a race of about one hundred yards, I was leading when the girl behind me threw up her arms and shouted for help. I went back to her and she immediately started to swim like mad in an effort to win the race! I realized what a dirty trick she had tried to play on me and was spurred on to make an even greater effort than hers and just managed to beat her. I vowed someone else could rescue the next person who tried this trick on me!

When we moved to Headington after Brighton, I went to a newly opened school called Headington School for Girls, a few hundred yards down the road from our home. There were only twelve girls there when Dene, Hazel and I started. One had to have an impeccable pedigree to gain admittance and we were definitely at a disadvantage since, owing to the very little money my mother had been left, we could not afford to wear clean blouses every day, or to have blazers bought for us like the other girls. As a result we were very much looked down on by some of the other girls and a few of the mistresses. The headmistress was terrifying. Her hair was cut like a man's and she would descend on us at great speed with her flowing gown if she happened to catch us doing some-

thing wrong, such as walking on the grass. I was frightened of her and she certainly did not class me as one
of her favourite pupils. At this time, I had an old pony
called Tommy and I spent all my spare time with him
rather than doing my homework as I should have been
doing. Not only did I come to school probably smell-
ing of the stable but my mind would wander to
Tommy instead of concentrating on the subject I was
supposed to be taking in. My reports were always the
same: "Barbara will only work if the subject interests
her," and with the exception of geography and botany,
the subjects did not interest me. Well, surely it was the
duty of the teachers to make the subjects interest me;
it was their failure, not mine, which showed up clearly
when in later years I went to college and gained very
high marks in all the exams. Why? Because the subjects
were put over in an interesting way and I was not
treated as a substandard object.

I feel this in the training of dogs. People are forever
telling me that their dogs are impossible. Their dogs
are not impossible; it is the owners who are difficult.
If the dogs are interested in the work they are being
taught, they carry out the exercises with gaiety and
pleasure, and give deep adoration to the teacher. If the
owners are drab or do not believe their dogs are good,
they lose the rapport with their dogs and achieve nothing. Praise and admiration are the greatest beautifiers.
That is why people in love have such a radiance; they
are being uplifted by beautiful thoughts and words. I
often think, had I received a little praise at school

instead of perpetual scolding, I might have done some good. I left school at the age of sixteen, heartily glad to say good-bye to my days there. Some years later I was most surprised to be asked to donate one pound for the provision of a chair with my name on it, so I suppose the existence of my name, along with hundreds of others on the chairs in the Assembly Hall, will remind people that I did at one time have some sort of education!

At the age of fourteen, before I left school, I secretly entered myself for the Harper Adams Agricultural College without my mother's knowledge. However, when I left school, they could not take me for another twelve months so my grandmother generously offered to pay for me to go to a finishing school in Switzerland for a year. My grandmother was a funny mixture of love and haughty dominance. She lived in a hotel in Paris in the Champs-Elysées, after losing her home and belongings to the Russian revolutionaries and after the death of her husband. She still had, however, a very large personal income which she lavished almost entirely on destitute princes from the Russian revolution. She bought them taxis so that they could earn their living in Paris. They all adored her, though whether it was ingratiation we shall never know. They were at her beck and call wherever she went. Even when she met me at the Metropole Hotel in London, a prince was hovering in the background, waiting for my departure. Actually this was my first and only meeting with her. I was thirteen years old and it was a devastating experience. I went at her invitation to lunch. When we sat down to eat she took one look at me and exclaimed, "You are hideous!" She then gave me half a crown and told me to go to the zoo—I am sure she felt the hovering prince could not meet such an ugly child! In fact I already knew that I was ugly for I had once overheard my mother saying to Nanny, "Why can't Barbara be pretty like Dene and Hazel?" I was not meant to have heard this but I think that is the reason I turned all my love to animals. They did not care what I looked like.

My grandmother never wanted to be called by the name Granny so we all had to call her Myth, goodness know why! I do not like my own grandchildren to call me Granny or Grandmother so I ask them to call me Granmummy, which I like.

After Myth had offered to send me to Switzerland, we obtained a lot of brochures from Truman and Knightley, the scholastic agents, and studied them carefully. The brochure that sounded most attractive was the one giving details of a school in Lausanne, Switzerland, which was owned by three sisters. It promised a first-class finishing school education in languages (which I loved), winter sports, riding and much else.

Before going there for my first term, my Aunt Claire from Scarborough had offered to send me on a winter sports holiday with the Children's Special Service Mission, which apparently specialized in taking three hun-

dred girls and three hundred boys skiing, adding as a
bonus religious instruction. Only well-brought-up children seem to have been accepted and the boys were
strictly segregated from the girls in different hotels and
were forbidden to meet the girls during the winter
sports activities. Unfortunately, on the long train journey, I met a boy from Eton, Robert Raphael, and fell
hopelessly in love with him. Rules about segregation
were ignored and I went skiing with him on the glorious slopes of Engleberg. I had never skied before and
was in seventh heaven when he taught me. As bad luck
would have it, a photographer, one of the many who
take photographs and put them in the local shop hoping for sales, took a photograph of Robert and me on
the slopes, and who should see it but a housemother
in charge of us girls. I was commanded that evening
to go to her room, where a sort of tribunal of
housemothers and an older girl greeted me; it seemed
almost like a court. They asked me why I had dis-
obeyed the rules and threatened that, unless I promised not to do it again, I would not be allowed out
by myself. They even asked me whether I knew Jesus,
and was I saved. It staggered me that I, who had two
brothers and had been brought up in a boys' public
school, should have been considered a sinner for having harmlessly skied with a very nice young boy of
about seventeen, my own age. I replied that my father
was a clergyman and our Christian upbringing had
been very strict, that I saw no harm in what I had done.

And I am afraid I went on meeting Robert. Alas, the holiday came to an end. He went on to Chillon College while I went to my finishing school and a term of absolute hell.

The school had a lovely view of the valley and Lake Leman. There were twenty-six girls, two Swiss teachers and a newly arrived English teacher. We were made to work very hard, having French crammed into us all day long, from six-thirty A.M. to nine P.M., with the exception of mealtimes, and with one hour's break in the afternoon when we went for a walk. We were utterly starved and my weight went down substantially. Then I became ill. My face and neck swelled so that you could not tell my shoulders from my face, and nobody seemed to know what was wrong. I was kept in my bedroom. Nobody came near me and no food was given to me except for two glasses of milk a day because the swelling caused my jaws to be clamped together. I managed to get a girl to post a letter to my mother, who did not realize from my description of my illness that I had mumps, and she got in touch with my grandmother in Paris. Myth asked her doctor to come to Lausanne and see me. He duly arrived, opened the door, exclaimed, *"Mon Dieu, les oreillons!"* and fled, worried about what his patients in his fashionable practice would do if he caught the mumps. After about three weeks, my swelling went down and I was allowed out of my prison. I had tried to write to Robert at Chillon but he never answered. When I was well, he invited me out with his mother who had come from England to see him and we had tea in Lausanne, the first good meal I had had for weeks.

Our letters home telling our parents how unhappy we were never seemed to arrive. We never went to winter sports and the nearest we got to fulfillment of the promise of sport was skating on the local reservoir with the Swiss teacher. She could not skate herself and we cruelly left her in the middle of the lake struggling to get to the edge. She was not a bad old thing, so eventually someone went and helped her skate back to the bank. We did go riding once a week. This was the only time I was happy, as I was always given the friskiest horse, with which I had a great rapport.

One girl at the school had a nervous breakdown and could not stop reading her French Bible. All day long, she talked French to herself until we wondered what we should do for her. One German girl with great initiative got her family to send her large hampers of food, which she sat up half the night eating all by herself. I plotted to run away. On Sundays we were all taken to Lausanne Cathedral for the mid-morning service, and I reckoned the best thing to do was to get off the tram on the opposite side to all the others when it stopped and bolt for it. I did this and got a train to the frontier. Unfortunately, I had forgotten the mesdames had my passport. They had notified the police that I had run away and I was taken back to the school rather ignominiously, shut in my room and nicknamed *La Sauvage.* I only mixed with the rest of the pupils during lessons and then was ordered back to my room to stay alone as punishment. From my window one day, I saw the three old mesdames go out so I went to their study and asked the telephone operator for the English consulate. I spoke to the consul and described the conditions at this *pensionnat.* He sent up one of his staff who, on speaking to the English mistress and seeing how ill I was, arranged for all the students to be escorted back to London by a member of the consular staff. It took me some months to fully regain my health after this.

# Happy Days
# at College

The months soon flew by and the day approached when I was to go to Harper Adams Agricultural College. I was the only girl on the Agricultural side although there were girls in the Poultry Husbandry Institute a short distance away. I lived with them at the Ancellor Hostel and shared my room with a girl called Vera Ashmole, a descendant of the man who had founded the Ashmolean Museum at Oxford. We became devoted friends and I still correspond with her even after all these years. We used to write our diaries in verse every evening. Unfortunately, when I later went to the Argentine, my mother threw away all my college things, including my diaries, which I was very annoyed about as those were the happiest of days.

In those days, a girl at an agricultural college taking subjects like building construction and surveying, veterinary science and engineering was almost unheard of, but I revelled in it. I was with animals all day long, learning as much as I could about everything to do not only with animal husbandry but also with the growing and harvesting of crops, bookkeeping, the making of butter and cheeses and the care of fruit trees. It was a very comprehensive syllabus and I loved every minute. In the evenings there were entertainments galore. I took the leading lady's part in the college plays. I entered and won shooting and bridge competitions at college. Later, when I left, I played county tennis and hockey and also won the annual car rally in my 1923 bull-nosed Morris, against which much more modern cars competed; Vera acted as navigator. I managed to get the second highest marks of all the students by being praised instead of being cursed, figuratively speaking, as I had been at school. I was even trained at college in the secrets of the four-cylinder engine and, thanks to my sensitive fingers and keen ear, I have always been able to tune the engines of all our cars.

I have a very keen ear for anything that is wrong with a car and used to offer my services to the local motor company to run their new cars around the block and tell them what was wrong with them so that the customer pre-delivery service would be more efficient. I could not believe that their business would not increase enormously if they sent out cars that did not spend their first two or three thousand miles on the road going back for repairs, which I am sorry to say is what happens with most cars today. However, the answer to my suggestion was, "Oh, no thank you, we would never make any profit if we put right all the things you would find were wrong," which is a sad reflection on the motor manufacturers. I have spent a vast number of hours of my time arguing with these manufacturers. I do not see why, when I buy a new car, I should have perpetual trouble. I fail to see why I should believe the customer relations chaps when they say that my car is "standard" with all the faults I find in it, and I utterly fail to see why the cars should not be made to stand up to their guarantee which is part and parcel of the deal. You would imagine that when these engineers are sent from the factory to try out one's car, they would realize they are not talking to someone who does not know a big end from a baby's bottom, and that the word "standard" must be a red rag to a bull when there can be no such thing as standard.

I will give you a perfect example of this. I once bought a new car which gave me trouble from the day it came. I have never had to fight so many battles as I did with the garage or the plant customer relations department to get everything wrong put right. In the end they agreed to do something they very seldom or, according to them, never did: take the car back into the plant and put it right. For the three weeks they had it I insisted they lend me a plant car. This they did, a much older one than mine and a much cheaper model. Never have I enjoyed driving anything so much. It never gave me a day's bad motoring; it was fast, silent, easy to handle and cheap on gas consumption. When they said my own car was ready, I suggested they give me one hundred pounds back and let me keep the two-year-old car instead of my brand-new one. This they would not agree to; all they would offer me was to take my new car in equal exchange for their old one, which I would have been crazy to accept. I never got the new one to my satisfaction and sold it when it had under three thousand miles on it. This company has lost my business. I expect they said good riddance when I was out of earshot, but I wonder really whether this type of incident does the car industry any good.

I am constantly told that I am an exceptional person, that most drivers know nothing about cars and that, to hide the noises, they put on the radio and drive the car until its collapse seems imminent. I try to explain that I love cars, that I have rallied them, that I have learned a lot about their insides and treat them with loving care. I hate to hear an engine running roughly. I cannot bear squeaks and rattles, or a gear box that resists the gear change. I should hate to have an automatic; it would deprive me of one of the greatest joys of a good car, a faultless gear change at any speed. The tuning of a car so that, even at quite high speeds it gives good gas mileage, is something that is possible with nearly all makes and to achieve this, one has to spend hours getting everything just right. I have often seen surprised motorists stare at me when I am looking under the hood, wondering if they should stop and offer assistance to the poor woman in distress; but running a car and tuning it on the road is the only way,

I believe, to get the best out of it. I remember once a factory engineer came and tested a car of mine whose gear box I complained was falling to bits. He tested it and said it was perfectly all right. Thirty miles later and twelve hours after his test, all the tabs fell off and we had to install a new gear box. I bet his company was pleased with him!

After carrying out experimental work for the Ministry of Agriculture, I left the college for good and have only been back once, long after I had married. The only memory anyone will have of me is the photograph in the Entrance Hall of all the students in 1928, which shows me among a sea of men.

College days were as happy as any young person could wish. The men treated me like gold and I had their respect. I remembered my mother's teachings so that although I had lots of flirtations, nothing really very serious came out of them while I was at college. Mother had always said that love should be treated like porcelain china, taking the greatest care not to harm anyone or break anyone's heart. Love is something that can make or mar one's whole existence. She insisted that we never lead any young men up the garden path. Men get their passions so easily aroused, she would say, that it is unfair on the girls' part to encourage them and then leave them cold. If men admire or love someone, their affection must always be treated with the greatest kindness and, even if it leads nowhere, they should remain friends. She said the chucking of boyfriends was something that only occurred in the servants' hall. This may sound very old-fashioned today, but to me it is good advice. These days young people change their boy or girl friends like their underclothes, with little feeling for the broken or cracked hearts they leave behind. Friendship hardly seems to exist. Love, often in its crudest form, seems to be galloped into headlong without paving the way with friendship first, and without finding out that true companionship is an essential of true love long before sex comes into it. This attitude, I am sure, has been aggravated and encouraged by television and newspapers, which only bring up the sex side of two young people's lives.

Nobody ever told me anything about sex. I knew from animals roughly what went on in the human race, and I was not curious to find out any more until I had married the man I loved. Men must have found me peculiar in that I did not wish to be kissed by every young man who brought me home after a dance, and if any man did kiss me on my doorstep with more passion that should be shown except in the privacy of one's marriage bedroom, he was out there and then. I kept my kisses for the people I had affection for. At college on the agricultural side, I was the only girl among sixty men. Had I been too easy with my affections life would have been less fun, as between the ages of sixteen and twenty young men are at their most amorous. I loved every minute of life at college. I spent most evenings walking the countryside with one

or another of the students there. We learned about life
in a nice way; I had lots of mild love affairs, lots of
proposals of marriage—even one from a member of
the staff who had never been closer to me than behind
a desk, but he proposed to me in a wonderful letter,
saying he wanted me as his wife because I was always
laughing. I can think of more sensible ways of choos-
ing a wife, but I was deeply honoured, and, I hope,
wrote him a kind refusal. I think perhaps my rather
old-fashioned treatment of men's advances intrigued
them. They used to propose to me with letters accompanied by huge bouquets of flowers or extravagant
boxes of chocolates, and my sister would giggle over
the letters, while I would feel sad for these men, so
obviously unsuited to being my mate. Usually the
weaker types were those most strongly attracted to me
and my way of life. I would have been a sort of life
insurance to them, I suppose, carrying their burdens
and smoothing their way, yet they were not my ideals
at all. I loved good looks and height. I had always had
beautiful animals and I certainly wanted a good-look-
ing husband, but it was kindness and gentleness and
the love of animals that I looked for, or rather hoped
for, because I never looked for men; they were just
beings that entered my very busy life and gave me
infinite pleasure in their company.

I corresponded for over twenty-five years, long after
I was married, with lots of my former young men.
Some were stopped from writing to me when they

themselves married and their wives were jealous; why, I cannot imagine. Could they not see that had I wanted their husbands, I could have had them long before they came on the scene? But then I do not understand some women. Men and women have a lot to give each other, even in correspondence; you do not have to love or want each other for yourself, but simply need to share ideas and friendship—but then I do not have a dirty mind, so to me there is no harm in friendship. I have had wonderful men friends, wonderful girl-friends, and only life's business has kept me from seeing more of all of them. But when one is up to one's eyes in work and rearing a family, there is little time left for friends. Yet if I do by chance meet someone I knew fifty years ago I can pick up the threads just where we dropped them that long time ago. I am always thrilled to meet old friends and acquaintances. People whose dogs I have trained many years ago suddenly turn up with a new generation of dogs to be trained, and it makes me terribly happy to meet them again. Suddenly, through a woman's magazine article about me, I started to correspond with the girl who had lived next door in Ireland and whom I had not seen or heard of for fifty years. It gave me enormous pleasure to meet her again by letter after all this time. Another one from South Africa also got in touch with me through articles of mine in the same magazine and recalled incidents of thirty years ago when she lived for a time in my mother's house. Again, reminiscing was the greatest fun. It is a pity that so many nice people pass out of one's life—at my age so many will never come back. The past is fun to bring back to mind; the future always does not seem so bright. They say that as one grows old one's memory goes back farther and farther; if you meet people to reminisce with this can be proved or disproved.

# Not Quite Home
# on the Range

When I set sail from England for South America to visit friends in the early 1930s, I am sure that I had in me more of the pioneering spirit than even Columbus himself. I was going out to a country that I knew little about, except from the wonderful books of W. H. Hudson and R. B. Cunninghame-Graham (an English author and political leader who lived from 1852 to 1936 and who became a cattle rancher in Argentina). I had been warned that the *estancia* or cattle farm to which I had been invited had none of the comforts of an English home, and that there was no wireless there, or telephones, or anything of that kind, but that only thrilled me all the more. There were, of course, vivid pictures in my mind from the innumerable cowboy films that I had seen, and my mind's eye pictured stalwart men with six-shooters, and the inevitable cattle rustlers—but that was all the background that I had.

I travelled out on a cargo boat which took a whole month to reach Buenos Aires, and I soon decided that riding the waves was not one of my strong points, for the smell of the engines in our small ship, the constant vibration, and the indescribably horrible odour of the disinfectant blocks that hung everywhere in the lower regions turned my stomach, and I experienced none of the joys of the cruel sea. I was in fact horribly ill for almost the entire journey, although I was just able to emerge at the end of it to enjoy the unbelievable beauties of Rio, its mountains, the gigantic blue butterflies, the blue and white foam of the enormous breakers on its honey-coloured sands, and the majestic Copacabana. This formed a sharp contrast with the murky São Paulo I had seen on the way there, whose sunken hulks had lain off the coast for centuries as reminders of the terrible plague which had stricken the city, and which had made it necessary in the distant past to scuttle ships and burn homes.

Most of the passengers had gone ashore there to see a snake farm some two hours' journey away, but for me the sunken ships still held evil and, as I hate snakes anyway, I had seen no point in joining the expedition. We had now reached the River Plate, whose muddy waters need perpetual dredging to keep the channel deep enough for its shipping. There is something exciting in its ugliness, as if it were warning one to turn back now before it is too late, but soon the giant sky-scrapers came into view, and here we were at last in the country of my hopes and dreams. I had bought two canaries when we had stopped at Madeira, for I had felt they would be companions to me in the vast loneliness I was heading for; but I then knew nothing about a law which forbade one to bring more than one canary into the country—a law, I gather, intended to protect the country in some way from getting overrun with breeding canaries, though I fail to see what harm would come of it. The customs man was adamant that only one must come in; but still I begged and pleaded and finally they sent for an official from the Ministry of Agriculture who, armed with sheaves of documents, tried to work the problem out from every angle. At last, helped by a quietly slipped-in tip, he decided that as I was destined for the very far north where the canaries would probably die in any case, they both should be allowed to come in. I felt quite exhausted after this set-to, and was glad to see my host on the quay and to leave to him the task of clearing my luggage through the customs.

Our train for the *estancia* was due to leave at two o'clock, so we had just sufficient time to return to the hotel for lunch and for a quick bath. When I came to pay, I found I was short of money, and of course the banks were not open on Sunday, so I asked at the hotel desk if they would cash a cheque for me on an English bank, which without hesitation they said they would. This surprised me greatly, for I was a complete stranger there and they neither asked me for a reference nor asked me to tell them where I was going to afterwards. How times have changed!

Two o'clock came and the train left on our eight-hundred-mile journey up-country. Everyone had a sleeper for what it was worth, but the sanitary arrangements on the trains were too dreadful, and I was warned not to attempt to wash in the basin, for fear that it might have been used for other purposes.

We travelled much of the way in the dining car, as one could see out from it on all sides, and naturally I was anxious to miss nothing. For miles and miles the scenery changed little; small houses with patios, surrounded by orange trees, all the houses in the little streets being flat-faced and whitewashed, with tropical creepers growing up the patio supports. Everywhere people seemed to be resting, and I was told it was the siesta time, when the whole country stops for three hours—shops close, work stops and silence reigns supreme. I found this habit most annoying all the time I was out there, for I myself never developed the desire to sleep during the day, and on those occasions when I had to ride sixty miles to the little town to do my shopping, I thought it a wicked waste of time and money to have to book a room to retire to in the local hotel when all I wanted to do was to ride home as soon as my shopping was done, which in the circumstances I found it difficult to do before curfew.

After two hours in the train we came to a ferry, where we were kept waiting for ages. The train had to be driven onto the ferryboat for a five-hour journey upstream, but the army were on manœuvres and had taken away the ferry unexpectedly—just like that! It didn't seem to matter to them at all that the passengers were inconvenienced, or that the railway officials in Buenos Aires had not been notified of what had taken place, and I was to learn that this sort of thing happened continually. However, we set off eventually and were able at last to stretch our legs walking about on the ferry. The river was murky with great reeds growing on either side, and beyond it was flat and uninviting. Small native reed-thatched houses were scattered about, and in the distance we saw a few miserable cattle and poultry. I soon retired and slept quite well, only to be woken in the morning by the rattle of shunting as we were now once more on rails on dry land. I went to the dining car as soon as I could to see if there was any breakfast going, and there I got coffee and rolls, but in the meantime I was being eaten alive by flies. I had had no experience before, except for horse-flies, of flies attacking human beings, but this variety certainly did, and we spent most of our time swatting them and trying to evade them.

The country had now changed: one no longer saw houses and orange groves, but pampas as far as the eye could see, and just a single telegraph wire that ran along by the railway line. From time to time we passed little farmstead homes of mud and thatch, each with a Hornero, or ovenbird, nesting on its gate in its own little round house. I discovered later that these birds build their round-shaped mud nests with a corner to go around inside, in order to protect their eggs and their young from their natural foes, the only enemy that could possibly get around the bend being a snake. It was for this reason that I was warned never to put my hand inside one of these nests, for fear that a snake might already have taken it for its home.

My eyes were kept glued to the window on the lookout for beautiful horses, but I saw very few young ones, only a few elderly animals tied up to poles near the houses, with heads drooping, and resting their weary legs one at a time. Suddenly the air began to darken and a most horrible smell filtered up through the floorboards of the train; the engine seemed to be working harder than usual, yet we were making little progress. The explanation was—locusts! Millions of them had descended on the area and they were being run over by the train. This was causing the railway lines to get slippery, and although the gradient was only a slight one the train was now skidding hopelessly. The sun was already blacked out and the swirling masses of brown creatures were hitting themselves against the windows. A few of them got in—great grasshoppers they seemed—and one of them came and sat quite happily on my hand. The train by now was at a standstill and the attendant told us that we should have to stay there either until another engine came to help us or until the locusts moved on: this they would do when everything edible had been devoured, which clearly wouldn't take very long. We watched the inhabitants of a mud hut running around madly, banging tins and saucepans to try and save their little plots of gardens, but within half an hour every tree in sight was

Dene, myself and Hazel with some feathered friends.

With Hazel, sitting on the steps of St. Columba's.

Riding Pamela, Mother's black donkey.

Charlie on his sled.

My father, the
Reverend William
Blackburn.

6

My mother.

7

By the beautiful sea. 8

9

Dressed in the new outfits Nanny had made for us.

Our new home at Sandfield.

Left to right: Dene, myself, Hazel and Bobby at Sandfield.

12 Left to right: Charlie, Bobby, Dene, myself and Hazel at Sandfield.

Collecting for the Royal Society for the Prevention of
Cruelty to Animals.

Dene with the kiss-curl
that was then popular.

14

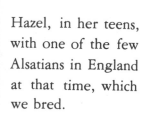

Hazel, in her teens,
with one of the few
Alsatians in England
at that time, which
we bred.

15

A Saturday afternoon outing with some of my friends at
Harper Adams College.

At a car rally which I won against
more modern cars in my 1923
Morris . . .

. . . and later outside my Wolseley
Daytona.

19

20

The tennis and hockey teams at Harper Adams—I played on both.

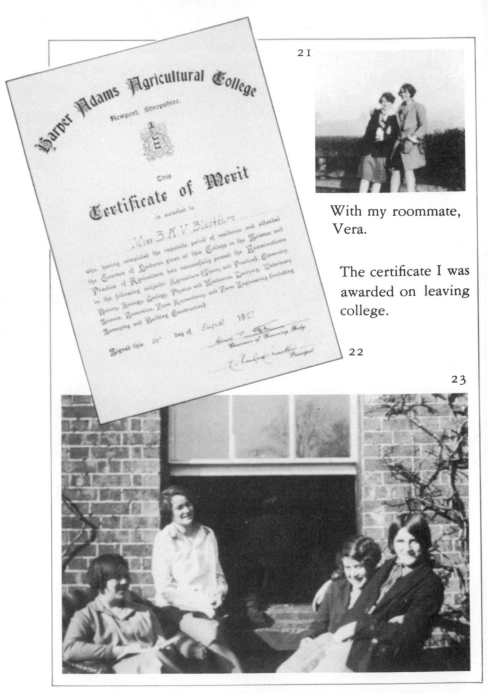

With my roommate, Vera.

The certificate I was awarded on leaving college.

22

23

During the college lunch-break with Vera, second from right.

Milking cows made me
an early riser.

24

Our *estancia* in
Entre Rios.

Breaking in Wendy,
who became a
trusted friend.

25

26

This photo of Jean and me was taken when I was twenty-three.

Riding a pony from the riding school I ran after leaving college.

28

29

My wedding day.

Judith.

Pamela.

30

31

32

Patrick.

bare of all leaves, and the whole place looked as if it had had a plague, as indeed it had. The locusts went as suddenly as they had come, and slowly the train started on its way again, carrying with it for some time the dreadful smell of burning locusts. After seemingly endless hours of the same monotonous countryside and evil smells, we finally arrived at our station, there to find our hosts, an English couple with whom we were to stay for that night; they had an *estancia* near the station. The hour was too late for us to complete the long journey by the rough roads that still had to be traversed before I reached my new home.

The *estancia* where this middle-aged couple lived belonged to the same company that owned the one I was going to myself, but it was a far superior one, the manager being an area supervisor and his *estancia* being used for the directors to stay in when they came out on official business and inspection. In fact it possessed all that one could need for comfort, with bathrooms, electric light, telephone and so on; also lovely buildings which housed magnificent thoroughbred stallions, and a vast number of beautiful brood mares that had been crossed with thoroughbreds to improve the native strain of pony. Here were pedigree Herefords, that were destined for the *frigoríficos* (freezing or cold store) and the frozen-meat market—the lean creolla cattle were bred for beef products and the tinned meat market. Incidentally they couldn't have used the gloriously fat Herefords for the canning trade, because the fat would have caused the tins to

blow. I learned this on my first visit to the factory,
where I followed a batch of our cattle right through
the process from *estancia* to shop. We all spent a most
pleasant and instructive day with these kind people,
and in the evening the men took guns and the manager's wife and I followed them across the camp, as the
land surrounding an *estancia* is always called. With us
came an old pointer bitch and her seven ten-weeks-old
puppies, which fascinated me by showing their hunting
skill at that tender age. Mother pointer flushed a partridge and stood immobile with quivering tail out-
stretched; and then all the puppies made a circle
around and pointed also, keeping quite still except for
their typically quivering tails. How I wished that I had
a camera with me, for it would have been a shot in a
million! What the partridge thought, when it eventually rose from this sea of dogs, I don't know, but it was
allowed its freedom.

Next morning we started on the last part of our trek
to the *estancia,* a wonderful old tin lizzie being our
conveyance. The Argentine driver seemed in an almighty hurry, and took bumps at such speed I was
often nearly shot out. Once we were going particularly
fast along a straight but bumpy road, when a partridge
suddenly got up and, in a fraction of a second, with one
hand still adhering to the wheel, the man whipped out
his revolver and shot the bird. He laughed, stopped
the car, picked the partridge up, and then with an
exaggerated bow handed it over to me. I felt that

66

whatever happened after that, I would never get on the wrong side of him or of anyone like him!

Some hours later, and without anything worse than a stiff neck and aching bones, we arrived at the *estancia* which was to be my home for some time to come. It was set in a lovely grove of eucalyptus trees; a windmill idled away nearby and, except for a large barn, no other buildings were visible anywhere, just pampas for as far as the eye could see. The house was long and low, with its inevitable patio. Some scruffy chickens and some Muscovy ducks with the typical red blobs over their noses were the only livestock in sight. I was told that the horses were all turned out some miles away in the camp, and that the peons (the equivalent of cowboys) were away counting the sheep and cattle of the *estancia*.

A wrinkled old Argentino came up and bid us good day, and helped us in with the luggage, and the old cook and her satin-skinned fifteen-year-old daughter came out to greet us, before we sat down to our meal of hard rolls and dripping jam. Butter there was unprocurable, the only people who ever made it being the Jewish settlers, who were the most industrious workers in the neighbourhood. It was impossible for us on our *estancia* to make butter because it was against the rules of the company even to keep a single special house cow, for it was ordained that all cows should be suckling calves. When we needed milk in the house, old Fernandez would go out on his horse to round up some likely-looking young matrons, and bring them into the corral with their calves; he would then lasso them one at a time and extract as much milk as possible from each unwilling cow. It was a risky business getting it from a wild and kicking cow, and sometimes it took eight or more cows to produce the half-gallon we needed. It seemed to me a most fantastically stupid rule, but out there company's rules were rules, and no one dared break them.

It was due to this stupid rule, as it happened, that I myself caught foot-and-mouth disease; for one of the cows that had been rounded up must have been suffering from it, and a human being can easily catch the disease after drinking milk from an infected cow. That is one of the reasons for the slaughter policy in Great Britain; but out there nobody bothers much about foot-and-mouth disease. Of course the cattle get it, and become terribly thin, but eventually they get over it and are then said to be the ones that fatten best. Very occasionally an animal cannot stand the fortnight or so of starvation and dies, but that is the exception rather than the rule. When I had it myself, I suffered greatly. In the human being the disease affects only the mouth, but great ulcers form on the inside of the cheek and soft palate, one's saliva runs just like a tap, and one cannot eat anything, but only take small sips of broth. I had to have a large rough towel tied under my chin, which got completely soaked in no time and had often to be changed, and I had to sleep as best as I could sitting up, or I should have choked with the persis-

tently running saliva. Everyone kept away from me for
a time, for fear of carrying the disease to the foreman's
little children who lived in a small hut nearby, for if
their new baby had caught it, it would almost certainly
have died. I recovered completely in about a fortnight,
and was very much thinner but otherwise quite un-
harmed. I can never catch it again, thank goodness!

After tea on that first day at my new home, I walked
around the house and discovered what a dreadful place
it was, without curtains and with only rickety old iron
bedsteads, with no fireplace in the sitting room, and an
antiquated bath. The latter consisted of an ordinary
bath indoors, connected with a pipe attached to a sort
of boiler outside. Whenever one wanted a bath, old
Fernandez was asked to fill the boiler with water from
the windmill; this, even using two buckets, took a considerable time to do, including all the walking to and
fro. Then a fire was lit underneath the boiler and so the
water for the bath got heated. It gave only just sufficient for one rather meagre bath, and old Fernandez
simply hated the job of filling the boiler, nothing putting him in a worse temper, especially as he saw no
reason for what seemed to him this fastidious behaviour. In the hot season, of course, we used simply to
ride out to the large windmill tanks that were situated
all over the camp and have a swim in them. They were
four or five feet deep and about eight yards across, so
one could have quite a nice cooling swim. The cattle
didn't much approve of our swimming in their drinking water, and used to stand with sad, disillusioned

eyes staring at us, and not daring to come very near.

Sometimes, in the drought, the cattle got too weak to reach the windmills, being so starved from lack of grass, and they would die by the hundreds from thirst. It was one of the saddest sights imaginable to see hundreds of sheep lambing down in a drought and having no milk at all to give to their lambs. It used to drive me nearly mad with rage not to be able to get milk from the cows to rear those lambs with; but my old cook and I did what we could, and we regularly had about twenty-five orphans, or *guachas,* around the house. But tragedy would come to us again when they grew up and had to go down in the company's counting of stock, eventually to be slaughtered. I think most people who love animals as I do suffer continually, for one's animals grow old so soon, or have to be killed like my lambs. I wish one could get hardened to it, but I never do.

Soon after my arrival at the *estancia* I went to look at the horses, and was given a little roan pony to ride. I revelled in his beautiful smooth action, all the ponies out there being taught the effortless canter on a loose rein, which makes it possible for one to travel long distances without fatigue. Their other pace is a very slow amble; by the use of long stirrups and neck-reining the horse, one does not rise to the trot, and this seems to be the perfect method of riding. I can never understand how English people can enjoy riding on their horses' mouths, with short stirrups and no neck-reining. But then, I have always ridden by giving signals to my horse with my voice and my legs, and by neck-reining for guidance.

The number of horses on that camp simply staggered me. There were over two thousand brood mares with their foals, and in addition there were the yearlings, the three-year-olds, and the *tropillas* or troops of working horses for the employees. Each peon or cowboy had twelve horses of a certain colour to use for the month that they were at work. At the end of the month those horses were pretty near skeletons and were turned free, and another *tropilla* was caught up. The peons were all responsible for their own horses and changed them about as became necessary. The foreman, or *capitas* as he was called, had the most beautiful horses of the lot. He was an expert at working in plaited rawhide and in Paraguayan silver. On his fiesta days, when he rode to town, he looked magnificent, silver on his spurs and on his bridle, and reins dotted with silver, and under his *ricardo,* or saddle, his horse carried a lovely patterned wool cloth made by his wife. I got her to make me one of these lovely blankets for my own saddle, for although I always rode with an English saddle, it was extremely comfortable for the horse, and a good protection for my saddle also to have a thick blanket underneath it. No horse ever got a sore back with one of these. They were made of unwashed sheep's wool, with all the natural oils left in, the colours coming from herbal dyes.

When I first went out, I was given three horses to use, and one was always kept saddled up and tied to our front patio, so that if I wanted to go out I only had to step into the saddle. But it annoyed me to be treated as rather an inferior being and not to be allowed to ride out into the camp with the men to see what was going on—but women were indeed inferior creatures out there. I plaited the manes of my three mounts, and pulled and bandaged their tails and groomed them all until they shone—but that didn't take up the whole day! So I would ride out into the camp to keep myself occupied; but it was boring riding broken animals. Soon I got a jump put up, and began teaching them to jump, and to play polo, and it wasn't long before these three knew almost everything.

My life out there at first was extremely tedious. The day started for the men in summer at about three A.M., for it was cool then for working the cattle. But I never got up at that time, as I shouldn't have had anything to do. I used to get up at about five-thirty, and take one of my ponies out for a ride, for that is the most beautiful time for riding out there. Everything smells sweet and fresh before the great heat drives one to darkened rooms and mosquito nets and the smell of anti-fly sprays. The flowers open early to greet the morning sun; and the colour of the verbenas, which grow in wild profusion on the camp, has to be seen rather than described for the full glory of nature's paint box to be appreciated. I used to return to breakfast alone; the folk from the *estancia* had eaten a stew or roast before they left and would not now be back until midday at the earliest, according to where they were working. I had no work to do because English women don't do work on an *estancia* unless they wish to cook; household help is cheap, and I was told at the very beginning that if I wanted even the matches off the mantelpiece I should call Maria to get them for me. She appeared to love to do things like this, and never seemed to object to being called for the most trivial things. I can't say I myself called her much, but the boss certainly did.

When I wasn't riding, or feeding my *guacha* lambs, or cleaning my saddle, I was left to do the only things I could do, knit or write long letters home. It was while I was sitting on the patio writing home one day that I heard what I thought was a motorcycle approaching, a racing motorcycle at that, the noise being that of one without a muffler. The dog jumped up and barked furiously; I stood up and anxiously scanned the horizon, terribly excited at the thought of seeing a fresh face. But it wasn't until the noise sounded quite close to my ear that I realized it was coming from the wings of a tiny little green and blue hummingbird, collecting the nectar of a flower growing up the patio. His wings were beating the air at such a rate that this fantastic noise was created. He was hovering, stationary in the air, with his beak in the flower head. I caught him and he didn't seem at all frightened; he was so tiny that his whole length was no greater than the distance from my thumbnail to my first thumb joint. I freed him and he again set up this loud noise as he set about his work unconcernedly. That is the first and only time I saw anything resembling him out there, and the next time I saw his species was in the Brighton Museum.

I used to ride again in the evening when the heat of the day was over. Life always stands still in the Argentine from eleven o'clock until two, or twelve until three, according to the season and sun. The heat is too great to do any work, and people who live out there soon get the midday sleep habit.

When the men came home at night, the evening meal was served, either outdoors in the shade of the tangerine trees or in the cool of a darkened room. All shutters are closed during the heat of the day so that the rooms may be bearably cool in the evening. We used to play cards most evenings, and I learnt to be most cunning over poker, though I refused to play for money. Usually I got left out of it as being a spoilsport. Bridge was the game we all liked to play most, but there were few chances unless English people came to stay, a rare and very welcome treat. Then we played all day and all night; tempers got frayed, mine not least, as I used to indulge in psychic bidding. I had beginner's luck, and seldom lost, although I should have done so according to the rules. I fear I never really liked cards, and the seriousness with which these games were played seemed silly to me. But I suppose when one has as little fun as that kind of life offered, these games become important.

I think I have shown how unvaried and purposeless life was until the time came when I was allowed to break horses for a living. To be happy while doing little beyond idling my days away was not easy for me, but once I had the horses to break it was a totally different matter.

It was now that I started pressing to be allowed to break in some of the horses myself, because for over a year I had had to satisfy myself with giving already tamed horses their extra schooling. That began to bore me, so I decided to learn to be a cook in my spare time. I had English magazines sent out to me by my mother, and in the weekly *Home Chat* I found enclosed a free gift of a cookery pamphlet having the interesting title of "Goodies for the Party"; so instead of starting at "how to boil an egg," I began at the other end with meringues and macaroons and walnut layer cakes, etc. I ordered a large box of provisions from Harrods at Buenos Aires, with such items as nuts, and rice paper, and glacé cherries, and much to the amusement of our old Indian cook, I set out to prepare dishes which neither she nor I had ever made before or even knew how to make. At first I found great difficulty in regulating the oven, since we had only a wood-burning range, and the heat of your oven depended on how much wood and draught you had.

After my first visit to the shops to get some fancy baking tins, I was quite excited at the thought of starting my very experimental cookery. "Beginner's luck," again, and beginner's luck my cookery certainly had. Everything we made from the little pamphlet seemed to turn out right, and thank goodness it did, because it was not long after our experiments began that, without any warning whatsoever, the English directors turned up to lunch and tea. Lunch is easy enough: a sheep or a lamb is killed, and an *asado,* or roast, is done on a spit outside. Everyone sits down with a knife and eats his or her fill off the knife, and there is little ceremony.

But I had different ideas. I knew that things had not been going too well lately on the *estancia,* a severe drought having caused serious losses in sheep and cattle, and the *estancia* was not paying its way as it should. I thought that if I could produce a tasty lunch it might mellow the bosses a bit. Fernandez had already been persuaded to make a vegetable garden behind the house and he had been quite successful in growing beans, and peas, and melons, so we decided on lamb chops "à la Milanese," which consisted of dipping the chops in vinegar and then egg-and-bread-crumbing them and frying them lightly. In addition we had potato chips and young broad beans. Then there were meringues, filled with vanilla cornflour mixture as we had no cream, and the meal was finished off with a tiny melon for each guest, with coffee to follow. It would have served them right if they'd had to drink it black, with the silly regulations that they made about not having a house cow! I kept them talking as long as I dared, and flirted outrageously with a rather susceptible Argentine inspector who accompanied them, for I knew it was his knowledge, mostly, that was the be-all and sometimes the end-all of these jobs. Apparently everything went off as well as could be expected, and old Maria and I felt we had done our bit.

On my rare visits to town I had to have the faithful help and companionship of old Fernandez; we each drove twelve horses ahead of us and covered the whole distance at a slow canter. At every five miles or so approximately we would stop if we saw a *puesta,* or small outpost, and ask permission to turn a horse out until our return. This meant of course that every new horse we used did a distance of five miles further than the previous one, although we never actually rode one horse for more than five miles. The last one to be ridden actually had to cover the full sixty miles, and for this last hop I usually kept my favourite grey Arab mare, who was so smooth to ride that I could actually go to sleep on her as I rode. They all followed the bell mare in front until the last changeover, when the bell mare herself was ridden by Fernandez. Whenever I felt that I needed a little sleep, I used just to set my mare near Fernandez and she would keep up her steady pace alongside him, never faltering—I believe that our understanding was so great that she would have kept me on her back whichever way I leaned.

When we arrived in the town Fernandez took the horses to one of the local tie-ups for water, and we arranged to meet again at a fixed time and place. I was now left alone to do whatever I wished. Usually we rode back at nightfall, by the light of the moon, as it was cooler then both for ourselves and for the horses. It took about eight hours' riding to get there, having started at about three o'clock in the morning. This time, when I set off for town, I was asked by the manager to buy him a pair of pyjamas, and I thought that an easy task as the word is the same in Spanish as it is in English. I got on very well with buying the things I needed myself, and then went to a men's outfitters and general stores and asked for *pyjamas*. The assistant understood what I wanted and brought out some boxes. I chose a simple pattern, left the shop, and thought no more of the matter until I returned to the *estancia*. The manager then opened the parcel and held up the jacket, and to my horror I saw that that was all there was in the box. The explanation was that the pyjama jacket out there was the Sunday-go-to-meeting wear of the smart Argentino. He wears black trousers, or if he hasn't these, baggy *bombachas* tucked into his soft leather riding boots, a pyjama jacket, a scarf, and a felt hat, and no one in the camp ever dreams of wearing pyjamas for night attire. Did I feel a fool!

The time to see all this smart garb is on a Saturday evening, in the plaza of the little town. All towns have their plazas, and on these occasions the young men of the district doll themselves up in their very best and parade around and around. The señoritas do the same, but they walk around in the opposite direction, always in twos or threes, and it is in this preliminary inspection that the young men decide whom to ask to be their partners in the dancing that follows. In every small town national lottery tickets are for sale for enormous prizes, and there are very few people who do not take at least one ticket; these are usually for sale on the same day as the dancing takes place, for it is then that outsiders from cattle and sheep *estancias* come into the town with money to spend. I used to stay to watch the young peacocks strutting around and to see the dancing that followed—but not for long, for there was always that journey home to keep in mind.

It was not long after this that we had a terrific freak storm and whirlwind. I had never seen or heard anything like it in my life. Roofs just went up into the sky, and sheep into eucalyptus trees. It also caused a most unhealthy state of affairs with regard to a child's coffin that had been suspended high up in a eucalyptus tree, where the natives put children's coffins, believing that a child when it dies must not be buried under the ground where the angels cannot reach it. So they make a little white coffin, and the poor little corpse is battened down inside and hung up in a tree. This particular storm brought one of these pathetic little coffins hurtling to the ground, and the bones were spread around, which was considered a very bad omen indeed. There was much crossing of themselves the next day, when as reverently as they could they collected the remains together again and replaced them in the little coffin, which again they firmly fixed on high.

This terrific storm caused many unusual phenomena. All night the wind howled and the rain came down as in a cloudburst. But at dawn it stopped as suddenly as it had begun, and we all went out to see what damage had been done. The first thing we saw was a river racing over the gulleys where formerly there had been no river. And now we saw fish, great big fish, where there had been none before, the nearest river being thirty miles away at least. I can only suppose that the whirlwind had picked them up and dropped them for us, like the miracle of the fishes— that at any rate is how most people would prefer to explain it. We hadn't seen fish since we left England and it was the greatest possible treat to eat them now. I weighed the one I took in and found it to be six pounds exactly. We baked it, after consulting my cookery book, and served it with tartar sauce! And very tasty it was too.

Shortly after the storm, the foreman's little son came rushing up to say that all his pet rabbits had gone and that in the cage instead was a baby skunk. The mother had perished in the storm and lay dead by the cage. How that living little skunk got into the undamaged cage, and the rabbits out of it, was beyond our understanding. In the mother's pouch were two dead babies. Experts cannot account for a skunk with a pouch, and try to persuade me that she was a possum. But she was no possum: she had the bushy tail of a skunk and was identical with the skunk picture in Cassell's *Book of Knowledge*. She did have a pouch; I examined her closely.

Anyway, I took the wee mite from the boy and put it on an old dress in the oven, which was now only warm. I then heated some milk, and with my fountain-pen filler got a few drops into its mouth. In quite a short time it seemed quite perky again, and I decided that, as it was a pouch-living baby, it must have something of the same sort now, so I popped it into the pocket of the riding skirt I was wearing. I lined the pocket with cotton wool, in case of accidents, and for a whole week my baby thrived there. He remained in my pocket when I went riding, and I wondered how he liked the motion. At night I wrapped him up warmly with a hot bottle for company. But, alas, he escaped from his wrapping one night and got severely chilled, and all my loving care was of no avail in saving his life. I am afraid I wept unashamedly when I found him dead. He had seemed such a sweet little thing, holding on to the pen filler with his little paws, that looked so much like hands, and sucking contentedly.

Speaking of skunks, I learned from my old cook that if one gets up and rides out into the camp at sunrise, one will see the meeting of the skunks. I rode out to see this one morning early and sure enough I saw a fascinating sight, about twelve of them sitting in a horseshoe, with one old chap at the head, just as we used to sit around the leader when we were Brownies as children. The old skunk at the top seemed to be briefing his family in the work of the day. They paid no attention to me. I watched them for about fifteen minutes, when suddenly they all got up and ran down their holes. One day one of the *estancia* dogs got too near one and came home exuding a terrible smell. My baby skunk had been too young to have a smell.

The storm was followed by another calamity in the form of smallpox. An outbreak occurred some distance away and the unprepared natives died like flies. We ourselves got orders at once from the company to vaccinate all our employees. They sent us lymph from Buenos Aires, but no instruments to do it with; so I sterilized the scalpel in my manicure set, thinking that that would just about do the trick, if Fernandez sharpened it for me, and one by one I gave them a scratch and smeared it with lymph. Some days later a furious peon arrived on my doorstep demanding another scratch; he had had no reaction, and his pals had told him it was because he was not a strong and virile man. So I did it again for him, assuring him that it was just because he *was* a big strong man, while his friends were weak and susceptible, that it had not come up, and that that showed he was not very liable to catch the disease. And that quite satisfied him.

It was extraordinary the amount of medical work that came my way, considering that my only knowledge of it came from the three years I had spent at Harper Adams, where the curriculum had included a short course of veterinary science. But the people had great faith in an Englishwoman's knowledge of ills of all kinds, although they have a local *curandera* of their own, whom they call in when their women are in childbirth, and she was supposed by all to have a great knowledge of herbal cures. I don't know what English doctors would think of the native Argentine ways when their offspring are brought into the world, but they certainly wouldn't conform to our standards here. The old *curandera,* heavily robed in black from head to toe, comes and takes up residence with the expectant mother about a fortnight before the baby is due to arrive, and when the birth is imminent all the windows and doors are heavily boarded up and the house is made completely dark, except for one candle. Both the husband and the *curandera* support the labouring mother when her time arrives. After the birth the baby is not washed, but is just wrapped up as it was born, until the third day, when the shutters are taken down again. The baby is then washed at last, and the mother once more goes about her daily tasks. The old *curandera* stays about a month altogether and is treated extremely well during her visit, as a sort of insurance against future ills. I often wondered whether she herself ever washed or took off her black garments.

I referred above to the woman's "husband" helping during labour: but in the true sense of the word he is not her husband, as they have not gone through any marriage ceremony. The natives, where I used to live, choose their *compañeras* (wives) from a local family, and the taking of the girl home to their *puesta* constitutes in their eyes a binding contract, to which they remain faithful all their lives. I never heard of any man leaving his "wife," or vice versa, and they bring up their children together, just as if they were in fact married; for in their eyes and in the eyes of the world the children of such a "marriage" are just as legitimate as if their parents were married in a legal manner.

They have many children, who from an early age learn to ride horses bareback, and are accustomed to helping their father or to running messages for their mother and to do other small tasks. They all live together in the one- or two-roomed native hut with no division of the sexes at all. Even the old *curandera* joins in without worrying about the close quarters or about segregation.

When anyone is ill, they make a wonderful mixture of milk and sugar called *dulce de leche,* which is supposed to be so concentrated in its efficacy that the weakest patient can live on a very small amount. I was constantly offered this food by the foreman's wife when I had diabetes, for she thought it would do me good, but it would of course in fact have done me much harm owing to its high sugar content. Its taste is rather like that of fudge and honey mixed and its consistency is similar to that of honey.

The small children of the natives spend hours of their lives perched on orange-boxes on the patio, where they are put to sit by their mothers, who know that they cannot get down and thus get into mischief while she is busy doing her chores. I have often seen the foreman's two-year-old son perched on his orange-box for three or four hours at a time, with nothing to play with and quite silent—yet he was a bright and intelligent little lad. At the age of four he used to go off galloping into the camp on a small fat cow pony. The little girls had blankets on the backs of their ponies, which were kept in place by a surcingle; they sat sideways on their ponies, but succeeded in galloping about quite happily. How on earth they stayed on I simply don't know. Very often an old granny and a child would ride on the same pony together in this fashion. I never saw a native woman riding astride in the Argentine, for even if they have a *ricardo* they ride on it sidesaddle and without a pommel.

It is amazing to me how contented with their lot they all seemed—a visit to the little village once a month appeared to be all that they wanted. Their rations of farina and meat came from the *estancia,* and were handed out to all the employees weekly. Most of them kept little gardens, where they grew sweet potatoes, and they all had chickens, for which they grew corn, and many of them kept Muscovy ducks and turkeys as well. They all dried wafer-thin slices of meat on lines in the sun, just like hanging out the washing. The meat dried in the hot sun until it was almost like leather, and was then packed away in boxes with salt. When they wanted meat, and no fresh meat was being killed, it was taken out and soaked for a few hours before cooking, and it was certainly delicious. To me at first it seemed so wrong that the meat should be exposed to the dust and flies in this way, but, after I had tasted it, I decided that it was tender and quite delicious—and after all it was well boiled before use, being always eaten in a stew. Into the stew went sweet potatoes, *choclos,* or corn on the cob, macaroni and farina, the ground flour. The oldest member of the family did practically nothing else but sit with a long-handled spoon stirring the stew, which seemed always to be on the hob. The lack of green vegetables was counteracted by the drinking of the herbal maté tea, and they never otherwise saw green vegetables at all. We English people grew them, but the natives never seemed to bother.

I think the faith that the natives had in their *curanderas* was fading fast when I was there, for I found that the people so often came to me with their troubles, which I treated as best I could with the homoeopathic remedies that my mother had brought us up with. I remember one day one of the outpost men came riding in to me in a great hurry, saying that his baby was dying and asking for my help. So I got onto my horse, and sure enough the child had a temperature of over a hundred and five, and, as I thought, had meningitis. I knew that I must get a doctor to it really quickly if it was not to be too late, so I set off once more with Fernandez on the fifteen-mile ride to the doctor who lived nearest to us, who although unqualified was said to be very clever. But I had been told that he wouldn't come out except for me or the manager, and he seldom would. However, I arrived at his door and he answered my knock. He said that he would come for sixty pesos, then worth about three pounds, but that he wouldn't even put on his hat if I didn't pay him in advance. This put me in a quandary for I had no money with me and Fernandez had only a few pesos. So I begged and begged him to come, and promised payment just as soon as the *patron* (boss) got back. But no, he would not come. So in desperation I went off to a smallholder with whom I had talked horses once or twice, and he generously lent me the money straightaway. We all rode back as fast as our horses would carry us, and the doctor when he got there did a lumbar puncture that saved the child's life.

I often had to deal with terrible wounds in the horses. They would get kicked by another horse, or gored by steers, or sometimes torn terribly on the barbed wire. I used to stitch them up as best I could with an ordinary darning needle and boiled thread. I found that some got well quite easily with antiseptic treatment, but others would go septic. It was then that I learned from the natives to allow the flies to blow the wound; for then, when the grubs hatched out, they consumed all the diseased and foul matter. At first this sounded to me simply too dreadful, but I tried it out in desperation with a horse whose skin on its face had been torn away and was flapping over its nose, after it had caught its head between corral bars. I had stitched it back into place in the way I practiced at first, but it had gone septic, so I opened up a stitch or two and in the hot sun the flies obligingly laid their eggs amidst the wound's smelliness. After some days the grubs hatched out and ate the wound clean, as the natives had said they would, and I was able to close it up again, beautifully pink and clean, after washing all the grubs out with disinfectant, and the wound healed quickly and almost without a scar.

One of the most frightening experiences I had was

once when I was alone on the *estancia*. Fernandez was taking the big stallion out to drink, as it was always shut up in the barn, normally, in the foaling season. Suddenly it bucked; he dropped its rope and it bucked again, kicking him full on the head. He dropped like a stone, and I saw that his skull was fractured at one side. I ran to the house for my cook as fast as I could, and together we carried him in to bed. I then pushed the protruding pieces firmly back together again and applied a pad of homoeopathic tincture of calendula which was all that I had. We didn't expect the men back for days, so I couldn't go for a doctor, for I knew that it was never safe to go off the camp alone. About twenty-four hours later he recovered consciousness, and I continued to nurse him for about three weeks, when he became well enough to go by borrowed car to hospital, where they X-rayed him and did a lumbar puncture. They soon reported him perfectly all right again, and I thanked God for his stamina and for the success of my humble efforts.

# Horse Breaking without Fears

To anyone who has not been to South America, to one of the bigger cattle *estancias* out there, it may sound fantastic that anyone should have a holding covering a hundred square miles, that took a week to ride around. The one I was on had sixty thousand head of beef cattle that had been trekked from the north to the fattening grass of our *estancia*. These were creolla cattle, long-horned and thin, but with terrific stamina. Most of them had been half-starved all their lives, and had to be acclimatized to the lusher pastures further south. They also had to learn not to eat the poisonous "Mio Mio" plant, which did not grow in the place they had come from and to which they were not accustomed. To teach them, they were put in a corral and a great quantity of the plant was burnt around them all night. The smell of the smoke so created seemed to give them a hatred of the plant itself, and they were then safe to be turned loose in the camp. Cattle that have been reared on an *estancia* where the plant grows do not need this immunization, but graze happily among it and never touch it.

A curious sight for the newcomer to the pampas is the way the natural roads are always in waves, absolutely parallel and regular. This is so because the cattle that are being trekked south always step exactly in each other's footsteps. The mud bakes in the sun and the roads stay like that forever. They become quite impassable for other traffic, so any motorists have to pioneer their own road nearby. These roads can be extremely dangerous, for directly the rain comes they turn into a morass in a matter of minutes, and if you are driving a car you can be up to your axles and completely stuck in a very short time.

I well remember getting caught like this when, after many years of having to ride sixty miles or so to do my shopping, we invested in an old Buick. In great excitement we set off to meet some English neighbours in a town about a hundred miles away. The weather looked perfect and the natives gave us no warning of impending storms. But perhaps this was deliberate, for they saw nothing but evil in the car we had bought. Anyway, at about six o'clock in the evening, I felt a queer premonition that it was going to rain and, in spite of the fact that the sky looked clear and everyone laughed me to scorn, I insisted that the menfolk from the *estancia* should leave their drinking and start for home. Many rude remarks were made about what a nuisance women were, but I ignored them all, for I was becoming intensely nervous, foreseeing danger. We hadn't gone more than twenty miles on the way back when I was proved to be right; the sky darkened, and soon the night became full of the most glorious coloured lightning imaginable—mauve, red, yellow, blue, and green—distant thunder boomed and growled, and enormous spots of rain spattered our windscreen. We were miles from anywhere, with open pampas as far as the eye could see, without even a native mud hut. I myself was driving, and I put my foot down as hard as I dared. The nearest village was San Salvador, some ten leagues (approximately thirty miles) away, but I knew we had no hope of reaching there, for the roads even then, with the spotting rain, were becoming greasy. The clouds raced up, the thunder roared, and at once down in a cloudburst came the rain. I skidded furiously, trembling with fear; the car became unmanageable and slid to a stop with its nose over a nasty drop. We got out to find the mud already up to the axle, and we soon realized that without horses to pull us out we should be marooned there indefinitely. We had no food, and we were shivering with cold. It is amazing how cold it becomes when it rains like that. The thirsty ground can clearly be heard ticking quite loudly as it drinks and expands. Two hours passed, and I said rather nasty things about not listening to a woman's intuition. The men were ominously silent, worried as to our future as the car sank lower and lower in the mud. Just as we were wondering whether one of the party should set off to see if a native hut could anywhere be found, three men rode up on horseback. We told them of our plight and offered a large reward if they could tow us with their horses to any sort of safety. Luckily for us they said that about a league down the road was a little *puesta* where we could shelter. The three horses had their lassos tied onto the cart and tried their best to pull it out, but it would not budge. So the men left, and an hour later came back with eleven horses in all, with the help of which we were towed to shelter.

If one has never been in one, the squalor of a *puesta* is scarcely imagineable. The walls of the houses are made of biscuit tins opened out and nailed to a frame of wood; then when the rains come and the mud is soft the owners plaster the biscuit-tin walls with mud. The great heat from the sun bakes it hard and so the house is made. There is no chimney, but only a hole in the roof, nor any windows. The average number of people living in a ten-by-ten house is about eight, without counting the innumerable chickens and *guacha* lambs.

It is the custom of the Argentinos to take innumerable sips of maté tea throughout the day. This is made in a gourd, with a silver *bombilla,* or pipe, to drink from, and every visitor, out of courtesy, must take a sip in turn. As the gourd is passed around, boiling water from the smoky fire is added after every sip, which I think prevents the spread of disease, for I cannot imagine a more certain disseminator of germs than this ghastly habit. Here then was I, faced with taking sips of this hateful stuff or offending our hosts. But, luckily, when it was handed to me one of my friends saved the situation by saying that I had only just come from England, where we did not drink maté, and would they excuse me.

It was already late, so we dossed down in indescribable filth and stench for one of the worst nights I have spent in the whole of my life. Darkness is an invitation in itself to all the millions of *bichas,* which include mosquitoes, beetles of every known variety, and all the other creeping things, and I was "the target for tonight"! Perhaps I was not as immune as my tougher friends who had lived out there for many years, and there certainly wasn't an inch of me that hadn't been sucked or tickled by these bugs when dawn came and the making of the fire drove the creepy-crawlies of the night to retire and digest their spoils.

As dawn broke the rain stopped, brilliant sun came out, and I saw a sight that I shall remember to my dying day. The pampas had turned pink as far as the eye could see, with millions and millions of autumn crocuses. Their leafless beauty had turned the drab yellow pasture into a picture more beautiful than anything I had seen before. But in a few sad hours the hot sun had burnt them up.

We sat down to breakfast on a stew, or *guiso* as it is called, with *choclos* eaten off the cob. Afterwards the men went forth to rally more people to help to get us on the move again. They reckoned it would take thirty horses to do it, pulling in relays. We got home finally after eight hours of travelling and the death of one of the horses from heart failure. The going was more than a foot deep in sticky mud, and never have I seen horses so cruelly overworked. My pleas of mercy for them were ignored, for the people out there treat horses like machines and when their working days are over, leave them to die by the roadside and to be devoured by the vultures. Many times I have pleaded without success for a bullet to be put in the brain of a moribund horse. Unfortunately, if one did it oneself, one would be liable to a heavy fine or imprisonment for killing somebody else's animal.

For a lover of horses the Argentine is the saddest place to live, for these most intelligent and willing animals and servants of humankind are never treated as they should be, but are roughly handled from the first. I think I learned to speak fluent Spanish more quickly than usual because of my rages—as when, for example, I saw a brute of a man knock a horse's eye out with one lash, and then laugh. I learned to upbraid such people in no mild language; but all they said was that horses were worth only a few pesos, and they must be taught quickly. Hence the cruel method of breaking a horse in, by lashing it to make it gallop and then pulling it fiercely back onto its haunches, three men and horses all putting a concerted pull on its mouth at the same time. I pleaded with them to be kind, but it had no effect, so I decided to show them that I could break horses as quickly and as well as they could and without any cruelty. I begged the manager of the *es-*

*tancia* to let me have a three-year-old to start on, but he refused point-blank. "Women don't break horses out here; that is a man's job," he said, and all my pleading fell on deaf ears.

But, as I said earlier, I don't believe in being defeated in anything I really wish to do, so I bided my time. Shortly after this the whole of the unit went many miles away out into the camp on a branding job and were away for three days. The only people left were myself, my old Indian cook, and the old native who chopped our logs for us and did all the odd jobs such as butchering. I saw the men off, and then went out to the barn to find old Fernandez. I think he liked me, for I was the only person there who treated him like an ordinary human being and not a slave. I asked him how long the *capitas* and *patron* would be away, and he said, "Three sundowns," so I told him that before they came back I wanted to break in a horse to do everything that their own horses could do. He looked at me as if I were mad, but listened to me when I suggested that we should ride out in the camp together to the wild herd and that he should lasso one of the horses for me. I promised him tobacco and pesos, and with much wagging of his head he agreed.

I could hardly wait while he ponderously saddled his fat old mare and went to fetch a little bay pony for me. Together we rode out and at last came to the herd. At first they paid no attention to us and we quietly rode around them. Then I saw what I wanted, a beautiful golden chestnut with four white socks and a blaze down her face. I pointed her out to Fernandez but he shook his head. "Don't have her," he said, "she has a *mala cara,*" which means a bad white face, and in the eyes of the natives suggests a bad bargain even before you start. But I knew this to be nonsense, and told him to catch her. Neatly the rope encircled her neck, and then she flung herself about like a salmon on a line. But eventually she was tied to the ring in the saddle of his own horse, and his old mount played the youngster like an experienced fisherman. Bit by bit she stopped pulling, and in the end we got her tied up near the house on a rawhide halter and a rope. By this time the old man was terrified of what he'd done and begged me to let her go again, for he said the master would kill him when he came home. I told him it was nonsense: that Englishmen didn't behave like that, and that I myself would take full responsibility. And in any case I had heard the *patron* telling him before he left to do all that I wanted. Miserably he slunk off to his barn to continue his routine task of scraping the fat and flesh off the sheepskins to make them ready for the tannery. I could hardly believe my luck. Here was this gorgeous creature for me to tame, and no one to say me nay.

I approached her gently, speaking in a low caressing tone of voice. She flinched at first on my approach and snorted furiously, but did nothing more. I then stroked her nose and her neck, and ran my fingers gently down her mane, for I knew that horses loved this, and soon she stood quite dreamily still; so I then ran my hands

Juno helps around
the farm.

Jyntee welcomed
by Judith and
Patrick.

33

34

One of the classes at my residential dog-training school.

35

36

Juno, aged six months, at her first show.

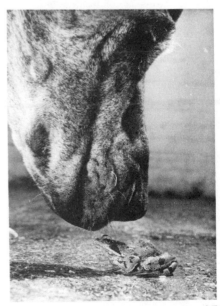

Juno talks to
our pet frog.

38

Juno learns police-work training.

39

Juno at play.

40

Juno at work.

41

Juno with Douglas Fairbanks, Jr.

42

Alec Guinness and Juno in *To Paris with Love.*

Juno with Clark Gable.

43

44

Junia, aged six weeks, waiting for a command.

45

Junia learns to be a clever dog.

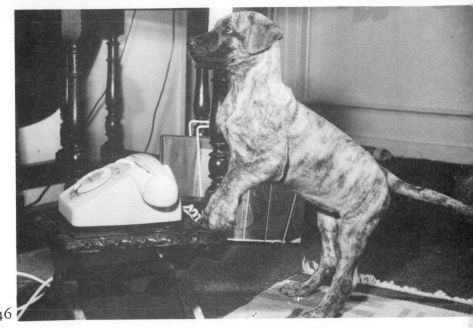

46

Junia hears the telephone ringing.

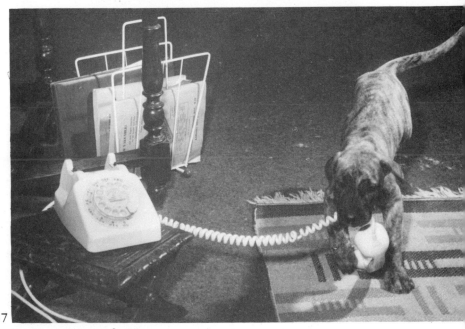

47

She answers it.

48

Junia records her howl.

49

Making a new
acquaintance.

Junia opens a cupboard to get her biscuits.

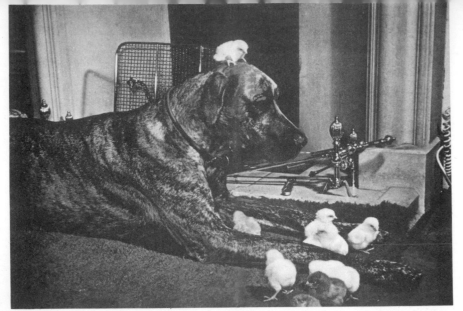

Junia and our baby chickens.

Relaxing with Michael,
Judith and Chica in the
garden at Campions.

53

Our current home, Campions.

Making
*Training Dogs the*
*Woodhouse Way.*

54

55

Junia goes to the studio in a Rolls.

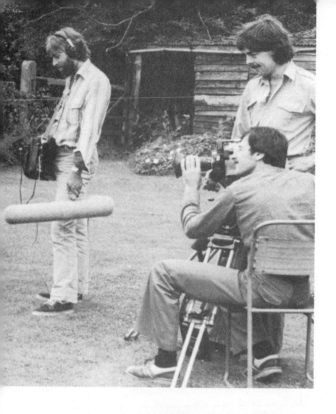

On *To Tell the Truth,* in New York.

57

Junia has her nails filed.

58

59

Above: A visitor welcomes me to a local fête, which I opened.

Another busy day
at the office.

Michael and I at Campions.

down her legs and picked up her feet, talking gently
and soothingly all the time. Next I went down her
body and picked up her back legs; then around the
other side and back to her head. Then I got a sack and
gently slapped her all over with it. She leapt in the air
with the first feel of it, but soon, when she found it did
not hurt her, she paid no more attention to it. I
whisked it over her back and under her tummy. I
slapped her legs gently, and down her tail. I then
dropped the sack off her back until she no longer
flinched, and that ended the first lesson.

Next I taught her to eat sugar by putting it between
her back teeth. At first she spat it out, so the next time
I held it in her mouth until it had nearly melted. That
worked wonderfully, and in no time she was crunching
up as much as I could give her. But I kept it as a reward
for everything new that I wished to teach her. I next
fetched my saddle and put it on her back with a very
loose girth. Up went her back in a terrific buck, but I
talked to her and moved the saddle about, and then
tightened the girth one hole and made her move. This
time she hunched her back but did not buck, so I
tightened it up to make it safe, and then got an old
wood block and put it by her side, so that I could stand
on it and lean heavily over her, talking all the while.
She never stirred, so gently I swung my leg over her
and slid on and off about three times like this. I then
put reins on the side pieces of her head collar, since I
do not believe in bits, and I sat on her back while she
was still tied up. Next I urged her forward a pace or

two, and then said "Ssh" and pulled her to a stop on the reins. Encouraged by her docility, I slipped off the rope she was tied up with and leaned over to pull gently on the halter to urge her forward. She walked on, and after half an hour of this I unsaddled her and took her out into the small paddock by the house and tied the long rope to a thick log and let her wander. At first she was terrified of the log moving along after her, but soon she got accustomed to it. After lunch I brought her in again and rode her for another half an hour. Soon she was trotting and walking well, but I still had the feeling that she might panic at any minute.

Anyway, to make a long story short, by the end of the three days this pony was going extremely well. I opened the gates of the corral, told old Fernandez to follow me at a distance, and off I went on her for my first ride. It was without incident for some time, until something frightened her in the grass, when she put herself into a series of bucks that would have done credit to a buck-jumping contest. I was ready for it, for all the time she had felt to me as if the slightest error on my part would make her try to get rid of me. However, we came home safely, and I caressed her lovingly and let her free in the small paddock near the house. Next morning I rode alone for an hour, and so her breaking continued smoothly.

On the last day before the men came home, I met an old Guarani Indian, riding a beautiful little bay mare. (The Guarani are a peaceable tribe of South American Indians, having their home chiefly in Paraguay and Uruguay and on the Brazilian coast.) We stopped and said polite things to each other, and I told him I was taming the chestnut I was on. He said he thought only his own tribe knew the secret of taming horses without fear, and, when asked what it was, he told me to watch next time I turned strange horses out together and to see what they did. I asked what he meant, and he told me that horses always go up to each other and sniff each other's noses, which is their way of saying "How do you do?" in their language, and that he always did the same thing when he wished to tame a horse himself. He said: "Stand with your hands behind your back and blow gently down through your nostrils. Keep quite still, and the horse will come up to you and sniff and will blow up your own nose, after which all fear will have left him. That horse, providing that you don't give it reason to turn vicious, will always be your friend and the friend of man." And with that he cantered off at the easy gallop of the perfectly matched horse and rider, with his reins hanging loosely and without a saddle, just a blanket on the horse's back.

That evening the men came home and I told them what I had been up to, and of course got the most severe scolding possible. Fernandez was threatened with the sack, but I pointed out that it was my fault entirely and that he had been ordered to do what I wanted. No more was said until I gave a little show with my *mala cara,* who behaved like a lamb, and the manager said he supposed I could break a horse. I felt

this was the moment to ask for another, for I was dying
to try out the Guarani's trick. So another was caught
up for me. I sniffed up her nose and immediately
stroked her and saddled her up. From her behaviour
she might have been an old horse, for she never
flinched or snorted or showed any sign of fear. I cut
out the preliminary sack-flapping and fondling and
gently mounted her, loosed the rope, and with my
heels urged her on. She went smoothly with me, and
I never for a second had that feeling I had had with the
other horse, that at any minute she and I might part
company. In twenty minutes in the corral I taught her
to stop, and to turn, and to trot, and then I asked the
men watching me to open the gate and away we went.
In an hour she was cantering, turning, stopping, and
allowing me to mount and dismount without any pro-
test or signs of fear.

I knew the Indian was right, for that horse never put
a foot wrong and in three days was a completely
trained pony. I could safely round up cattle with her,
open and shut gates, and so on; and all this on a head
collar only. I never bitted my horses until much later
on, when I knew that they knew what to do from my
voice alone. I have won many a bet in England that I
would do anything normal on a horse without saddle
or bridle, winning simply because I knew that my
horse knew every command of voice. For a bet, I have
played fast polo on reins of one strand of 50-gauge
cotton. My success with the Guarani's trick gave me
the chance in life I had always wanted, for from now

on, instead of the peon being paid to tame the horses, they were given more useful jobs, like fencing, to do, and I was promoted to be horse breaker at ten shillings per horse. The inspector of the cattle company was told about me and came out later to see why a woman was allowed to do this. He rode one of my horses that had been completely untouched two hours before and could find no fault in it except lack of experience. It was thus that I became the happiest woman on earth in my self-chosen job.

# Taming Horses in the Argentine

About three months after the inspector's visit, a letter was delivered by hand to the manager from the area manager instructing us to move that very day to take over another *estancia,* in quite a different part of the country.

Nothing pleases me more than to get a move on, but this unnecessary move without any warning struck me as being just red tape. Here we were having to gather up our entire personnel with all their worldly goods, all our domestic livestock, maids and their belongings, and set off to take over another *estancia* about eighty miles away! The manager, however, was delighted, for it was a promotion for him apparently, and the new *estancia* was much nearer civilization. The railway ran through it and there was a little village only a league away, so as far as he was concerned everything was lovely.

Our old cook wasn't too happy about leaving the place she had lived in so long, but she didn't think it would be right to leave me unchaperoned, so with much grumbling all her belongings went into a sack. Nor did her daughter want to leave her other unmarried sister who lived in the neighbourhood, so they were both invited to come along too. After all, they were paid only about five shillings a week each anyway.

Dawn was around three in the morning, and then hustle and bustle started everywhere. One could hear the clucking of frightened chickens and the fury of turkeys and ducks as they were all hustled into wooden crates and stacked under the great farm wagon that was to move the household. We had one farm wagon for the domestic side of the move and two more for the *estancia* essentials. They were huge wagons, each drawn by six horses, but in spite of their size they seemed to me terribly overloaded, and it was agonizing to see the horses struggle to get the wagons started.

I rode as usual with faithful Fernandez to accompany me. In the wagon were old Maria and her two daughters, with the foreman's wife and her three babies. Fernandez and I rode behind. The manager had gone on with the foreman, some hours before, on horseback. With us, all went smoothly for the first forty miles, but when we arrived at a river, the wagon driver, instead of asking Fernandez to go ahead and see how deep it was, just shouted for all he was worth and lashed the horses, who sprang straight into the water, which was far too deep for them. Within seconds they were swimming for their lives, with the wagon floundering hopelessly, and its occupants up to their waists in water even though they were already standing up. They were holding the babies above their heads, and the household goods were floating around everywhere. The horses succeeded in reaching the other side, but pull as they might they couldn't get the wagon up the slope out of the river. The driver thrashed them mercilessly until I yelled to him to stop and then plunged my horse into the river and snatched the whip from the brute's hand. He knew he was himself to blame and was venting his anger on the horses. I told Fernandez to go and get help while we did our best to keep the horses quiet. The wagon was safely grounded on the riverbed, but of course all the poultry that had been slung under it were drowning. I went back into the water two or three times to rescue floating articles, my Arabian Wendy appearing to enjoy her swim. It seemed ages before Fernandez returned with three men and horses to pull us out, his own horse being attached to the wagon with his lasso. What a sorry sight everything was! Every blanket was drenched, all the clothes the travellers possessed were wringing wet, and there were still about forty miles to travel before reaching the new *estancia*. I spoke to the men who had come to our aid, and they invited the cavalcade to stop at their *puesta* further on to dry out. It was sad to see all the dead poultry, and among them the two geese which had been real friends to me, though I fear I did not regret the foreman's turkey cock! He had been a vile bird and his angry red face had kept the other poultry and the foreman's dog completely under his rule for many years.

We rode on with the wagon and its occupants as far as the *puesta,* and then I left them, for I too was soaking wet, and it was by no means warm. It took us six long hours more to ride to the new home. We stopped only once to give the horses a drink, and an old señora rushed out to offer me her maté pot, which I dared not refuse. But I certainly said a prayer for the future state of my health when I drank from it! The old señor came out too and admired my Wendy. He said he would like to buy a foal of hers, if ever she had one, and then he asked me if I'd like to see his yearlings. I gathered that this was a great district for Sunday race meetings, all the neighbouring landowners competing, and he showed me one glorious bay pony that he kept in a tumbledown shack. It was bounded in by sacks, and he told me he fed it on maize and alfalfa and that it had won ninety races already. Had I not been so wet I should have liked to talk to him much longer, for he obviously knew a great deal about horses. But we had to get on with our journey, so I waved good-bye, and the whole family came out to wish us *hasta la vista* ("Until we meet again").

By this time I was beginning to get badly rubbed, with my wet clothes against the English saddle, and it made me appreciate the quality of the native saddles that they use out there. These consist first of all of a mackintosh covered with a woollen blanket; then two panels of stuffed leather kept together with leather thongs like a corset, so that the size can be altered to fit any horse. The pads fit snugly on each side of the backbone, and are covered with a natural sheepskin, and on top of it all goes a warthog's skin which is beautifully soft. The idea of these saddles is that a rider is thus able to carry everything that he is likely to need for weeks in the open. The mackintosh goes on the ground, when he is making his bed in the open, and on that goes the woollen blanket. Then the leather pads make his pillow, and his big poncho, without which no Argentine rider of the range would ever travel, finally covers him over completely. No rain, however heavy, ever penetrates a poncho. When a man is riding, if the weather is fine, the poncho is tied in a roll in front of his saddle; but if it rains it is worn buttoned high up to the neck, and used like this it covers the horse as well.

I was getting into a state of utter misery and discomfort, so I tried to ride sidesaddle for a few miles, a rather risky procedure without a pommel. However, Wendy knew that she had to be very careful, and it certainly helped me. At last we arrived, and the excitement at getting there made me forget how sore and weary I was.

The *estancia* house was on a hill and could be seen from some distance away, and the country was quite different from what I was accustomed to. There were wizened trees which bore flowers very much like mimosa and had an intoxicating scent. Parrots shrieked from the palm trees, and there were streams everywhere, shallow and easy to ford. However, the water in them is not always so low. There was one stream that ran at the bottom of the *estancia* which was a mere trickle on the day we arrived, but I remember that some months later, when we had a terrific storm, in a few minutes it had become a roaring flood. You can judge from what follows how quickly that happened. A traveller who was delivering a new car to a customer was passing through it just before the storm came, when the car stalled in midstream and the man got out to walk to our *estancia*—ten minutes' walk at the outside—to ask for a horse to pull him out. But by the time we were able to get a horse ready and get back to the car its roof was the only thing visible. The roaring raging torrent had widened the river to fifty yards and no horse could have lived in it. This spate lasted for three weeks and the car became a total loss.

Well, to get back to our arrival at our new home. It was late evening already, and I was hoping that the manager or the foreman would have got a fire going and a kettle boiling ready for tea; but when we arrived the place was just a bare shell. In this district, apparently, wood for fuel has to be brought from a long distance and the outgoing manager had left none. But it takes a woman to make a home, and in no time I had scouted around and found some old boxes and had got a fire going and a cup of tea ready. I had to dry my own things on me, as all the trunks containing our clothes were coming on the other wagons by a different way, and the wild horses were being driven along with them. I was glad they weren't attempting to come the way we had come ourselves.

This new *estancia* consisted of three rooms in the main house, and kitchen quarters and, joy of joys, a bathroom with a modern bath! Then there was another part which provided an office, and a very large room which the manager had for himself. The foreman's cottage was fifty yards away and nearly as comfortable as the main house. All around the house were tangerine trees and excitedly I picked the luscious fruits and ate them. They were much more delicious than any I had ever tasted before, and I ate many of them. On the house grew geraniums of all kinds, pink ones and red ones, and in the back there was a vegetable garden with everything in it that one expected to find in an ordinary English garden. My mind flew to the cookery book, and to all the things that I should now be able to make. But how much more I should have enjoyed my first sight of this new home if I hadn't been so cold!

Fairly soon after we had got there, the poor people in the flooded wagon also arrived; they were very tired, but surprisingly cheerful. I have never known more charming, simple people. Their wants were few and they became such faithful friends. Their first thoughts were for me, but I assured them that I was all right. Luckily I had the kettle ready boiling for them, and the foreman had slaughtered a lamb and a roast was being prepared outside. Soon they were sipping their maté, and before long we all settled down to the coldest night we'd spent for a long time. The blankets were soaking wet, and it wasn't until the sun came out next day that we were able to dry them at all. The first thing that old Maria and her daughters did next day was to go down to the little stream and wash everything that had got dirty on the journey. I went down to see what they were doing, and was astounded to see them pounding everything between stones in the running water. Then they laid it all out on the grass to dry, and never had I seen more spotless things, when they had finished! I shall never understand why everything wasn't in holes in a few minutes, but in the two years I was there I never saw even the finest underclothes in any way harmed by this treatment.

Old Maria's daughter Valentina used to amuse me by catching fish in the stream with her hands. But it did mean that we could always have fish for a meal when we wanted to. The fish she caught were delicious little fish and she must have pounced like lightning to grab them so quickly—certainly no one else could do it.

Just beside the river some distance from the *estancia* was a swampy area covered with very green grass, and it was here that we lost the horse for the sulky soon after we arrived. It was a horribly impressive as well as a saddening incident, for until I had this demonstration of the powerlessness of muscle and bone against the dreadful suction of the bog, I had felt, as many do, that by the exertion of courage and utmost physical effort, escape might be made possible. Our sulky horse was not as fortunate as the little pony whose adventure I am about to relate. This working horse had gone to graze in the lovely green patch, which looked so inviting after the burnt-up pasture he had been used to, but he met a terrifyingly quick death in the treacherous swamp before anyone could get a rope around his neck to pull him out. It was dreadful to see the helpless creature die in this way, and, as a good sulky horse is a rarity, his loss was also a tragedy for us all.

Apparently there were many such dangerous swamps, and, unless one can get a rope around the animal's neck quickly, a horse or a cow is sucked right under in no time. Our own horses came from a part of the country where these swamps didn't exist, so they were always having to be pulled out. I remember that soon after we got there, I was riding a pony one day that I had only just started to break, when without warning her back legs went down and we began to sink rapidly. My only hope of safety was to climb over her head onto some dry grass that I could see ahead, and then try to pull her out. Fortunately, she trusted me implicitly, and I prayed that she wouldn't struggle or our days would be over for both of us. She was sinking steadily, but did nothing as I climbed up her neck and over her head onto firm ground. Then I urged her to try to get out. I pulled with desperate strength, and she struggled valiantly with me, only resting when I did. Little by little we won through, and finally with an almighty heave she got her front feet onto firm ground and then pulled herself out. We were both of us gasping for breath and I was thankful at that moment for the bond of trust there was between us. She knew I would try my hardest to save her life and so she did just as I wanted. Slowly and carefully we rode home, and from that day on she was one of my favourite horses. I was sad indeed when later on the manager claimed her and gave her to a man to train as a racing pony. She was extraordinarily fast and won many of the Sunday races for him, but she was worth more than that to me as a mount.

That was the heartbreaking business of being official horsebreaker, for I loved them all and never wanted to part with them to the peons who treated them so differently from me. All my wages went in buying for myself as many of them as I could afford.

At this time I was taming about four of them every week. They were caught up from the herd for me, I breathed a welcome up their noses, telling them gently all I wanted them to do, and they submitted themselves to me almost immediately. I never spoke to them above a whisper, for I know that animals like a quiet voice, and if you are in tune with them it just doesn't matter what words you actually use. It is the intonation of voice that matters, and one's thoughts are transmitted in some mysterious way through the touch of one's fingers or directly from mind to mind. Time and time again I have proved this when out riding, by just thinking silently of which way to go, and finding that the pony almost invariably takes the right turning. It is very much the same thing when I am upset or angry,

for the animals always know without a word being
spoken when I am unhappy, perhaps, or ill, or if I am
out of temper. I now make it a rule never to go near
my horses to attempt to tame them if I am cross about
anything, for my irritability communicates itself to
them at once, and then that communion is lost which
is so essential if one is to make them do what one wants
them to do, instantly and without fear.

# Jean, My First Dane

Jean's life had only twenty hours to go when chance led me to meet her. I was staying with an old Oxford friend of mine at Hartburn near Stockton-on-Tees and he was invited over for drinks with some neighbours. When we arrived there I saw this huge Great Dane lying on a sofa and went over to talk to her. She instantly snuggled up to me and I asked how old she was and they told me six years old, but the sad thing was she was going to be put to sleep in the morning as her owners couldn't keep her. The present people she was with already had two other dogs and really couldn't have a Great Dane. Instantly I said, "Could I have her?" and of course they were utterly delighted.

I had only had Jean about six months when I accepted the invitation to go out to the Argentine to friends, my obsession being horses, and the thought of living with six thousand horses on an *estancia* I'd been invited to whetted my appetite for the wide open spaces.

But my first thought, when we had settled down in this new *estancia,* was to send for Jean, whom I had had to leave behind in England; so I cabled my mother asking her to put the dog on the next boat out, and saying that I would meet her in Buenos Aires, as we were now living only a few miles from the junction station and I could easily go down to meet her alone. I had not dared to bring her out with me, not knowing what I was coming to, for I felt that she would die when put into quarantine, if I had to return to England. This *estancia* kept more sheep than cattle and I looked forward to teaching my dog to work the sheep. She used to understand every word I spoke and I felt that with her I would have a wonderful time. It thus came about five weeks later that I left the *estancia* for the first time for over eighteen months to visit civilization once more.

I got to the docks many hours too early, and was tremendously excited when I saw the ship in the distance waiting to dock. When at last she came into the wharf, I could see Jean standing by the rail, being held by some strange lady. When I whistled to her she went nearly mad, and I thought for a moment that she would jump over the rails. It had been a silly thing for me to do, but I longed to make sure at once that she had not forgotten me. In no time she came down the gangway, and there was no holding her. She bounded into my arms, nearly knocking me down, and I got a complete bath of kisses. Then I noticed that she was lame on a back leg and I asked what had happened. I was told that a drunken sailor had kicked her, and I could see that although the wound had healed she was still lame, which worried me dreadfully. She never did get quite right again after that, but fortunately it didn't seem to bother her at all.

I took her off to the hotel where I was staying the night and she clung to me as if she daren't shut an eye for fear that I should disappear again. She was tremendously admired by everyone, for I don't think anyone there had ever seen a Great Dane before. I had to go to the railway office to get special permission to take her on the train with me and to get the train to stop at the *estacion,* the station, which they would do by arrangement in those days, as they had very few passengers. But to my dismay, when I got to the station, I found the guard most unwilling to have her on the train at all. I promised, however, to stay with her in the guard's van all the time to make sure she did him no harm, and this seemed to satisfy him. On the way, when we were on the ferry, I took her for a walk around it, and the dining-car assistants gave her a good meal of meat. Eventually we arrived at our destination and were met by old Fernandez in the sulky. Jean jumped up at once and sat bolt upright beside me, taking everything in, and every now and then she gave me a big lick on an unsuspecting cheek. It seemed as if she just wanted to keep on telling me how much she loved me! When we arrived everyone rushed out to greet us and to admire Jean; but alas, she wouldn't greet the manager, and so to him she was a stupid dog. I tried my best to persuade her to be friendly with him, but no, she dropped her tail, and looked miserable. Later I knew that she was right, as animals always are.

I soon taught Jean to be a first-class sheep dog and we took over some of the work with the sheep. It was good for the horses I was breaking to have some definite work to carry out, and Jean used to go down to the gullies to pick up any lambs that had fallen down, which she would then bring up in her mouth. Only a Great Dane could have done that. I used then to sling the lambs in front of me on my horse and take them back to the *estancia,* as most of them were found to be injured in some way or other.

One day, when I went out to the flock, a ghastly sight met my eyes. Some killer dogs had been at work and dead and dying sheep were to be seen everywhere. I knew that I must go back to the *estancia* immediately to get help, but if I were to leave the sheep unguarded the birds of prey would peck and kill those that were not yet dead, and the killer dogs might return. So I tried to explain to Jean that she must stay and guard them until I came back. She seemed to understand what I wanted, in her quiet way, and to show me that I need not worry she lay down and closed her eyes as if in sleep. When I went away, for as far as my sight would carry I kept turning back to watch what she was doing, and whenever I looked back I saw her beautiful head still held upright and that she was still watching me and never moving at all. It took me seven hours altogether to get help, for there was no one at home when I reached the *estancia* and I had to go out to find the men where they were working. I was much worried as to how Jean would feel in the terrible heat of the day, as she was not accustomed to such high temperatures, but when we got back eventually, she was just where I had left her, and I don't think she had moved more than fifty yards in the course of her duties. The sheep were grazing quietly, and those that had been hurt had suffered no further harm from the vultures. How glad Jean was to see me, and to have a drink and some meat that I had brought for her! I then left the men to their heart-breaking task of slaughtering the injured, and wound my own weary way home.

One day, as I was taking my siesta on the patio, I heard shouting from the foreman's cottage and his little boy came running up to say that the locusts were coming. Everyone panicked, shutting all the doors and running about banging sheets of tin or anything else that they could lay hands on. Jean thought it meant burglars, and I am sure that her bark must have frightened many of them away! But soon it became almost dark with them and the ground was literally covered. Towards nightfall the locusts climbed up off the ground and clung to the trunks of trees or anything else they could cling to, and the ponies ate them ravenously. Jean ate some too, but didn't seem to think them very tasty. It appears that locusts always climb up the trees in the evening, if they can, and their wings get wet with dew during the night's rest. They then descend again in the morning, when their wings are dry, and go on eating everything in sight. Our own plague stayed to lay their eggs, and soon there were millions more of them in the crawling stage. These the men tried to slaughter by digging great pits for them, when they were on the move, and then pouring petrol over them and burning them up. When we got rid of them at last the camp was seen to be completely bare, and the sheep with their lambs were soon in a desperate plight. The losses were terrible. It is a frightful thing in that part of the country, where no special crops are grown as extra food for the animals in an emergency, the cattle and sheep must starve to death if severe drought comes or a plague of locusts. On this occasion some of the flocks were sent elsewhere as quickly as possible, but the sheep were so weak by then that many of them died in transit.

It was great fun having a little village only three miles away, and I often used to ride there on my pony, with Jean for company, to do the shopping. I was always puzzled by the terror my pony showed when we got to a certain spot in the road about halfway there. She used to refuse to go on without much soothing and quite firm handling on my part, and Jean also showed her obvious uneasiness and her hair would stand up all the way down her back. I told the villagers about this and I found out that the road had been made through an old cemetery, and it was the ghosts of the dead that were supposed to be haunting it. This seemed to confirm the theory that animals have a sixth sense and can see things we ourselves cannot see, and the uneasiness of my own animals, when we passed that way, certainly made me feel very creepy. I think there must have been some exceptionally conscienceless evildoer buried there, for surely an animal would not be so deeply affected at passing a burial ground, if it were not haunted by some earthbound spirit—but one knows so little about what animals can sense and fear.

After one extremely hot day, we had all just settled down to our evening meal when all the *estancia* dogs set up such a noise that Jean leaped up to add to the furor with her own booming bark. We went to the door and discovered a cavalcade of horses, dogs and children approaching. There is an unwritten law in the Argentine, known as the "sun-downers' law," which makes it absolutely necessary to give board and lodging to any traveller who needs it from sundown to sunrise—and here our hospitality was wanted with a vengeance! The party consisted of an old father and mother and seven children, not to mention innumerable dogs and horses. So with smiles hiding our dismay at such an invasion we went out to greet our guests. We gave instructions for a roast lamb to be got ready and maté pots were soon steaming and the whole family making polite conversation around our fireside. It was as much as I could do to stand the smell of their unwashed bodies, not to mention the expert spitting into the fire of old papa.

The children were fascinated by my canaries, and before I could say a word the poor little hen had been frightened off her eggs. Her eyes and those of her mate became little black pinpoints of terror, and I had to take her into my bedroom and to speak soothingly to them both before the little cock would give me his usual bright "cheep, cheep." The little hen needed even more comforting, so I took her out of her cage and pressed her little beak to my mouth and kissed her, as her poor little breast panted up and down. This I feel is a bird's language: so many species caress each other with their beaks—perhaps it is a reminder of the nestlings being fed by the parent birds. She soon realized that she was safe, so I gently returned her to her nest. She then looked at me as if to say thank you, fluffed out her wings until she looked double her normal size, and settled off to sleep, and to dream of her future family.

On returning to the bedlam in the sitting room I found papa, with the help of a bottle of *caña* (a liquor distilled from sugar cane), becoming very companionable. His stories of his wins on the racetrack were becoming more exaggerated every minute. Mama was suckling her youngest baby, and the other children were still rampaging about. I made wild dashes here and there to save my odds and ends, but in the twinkling of an eye the inkpot was over the carpet, a picture came hurtling down, and Jean had slunk off outdoors. So I blessed the moment when the foreman announced that the meal was ready at last. Knives were then drawn from their sheaths, and the family went out to eat their fill. I myself said good night and expressed the hope they would sleep well in the office room which had been made ready for them. On the following morning, after many pretty speeches, the whole noisy family moved on.

So the summer passed. I was happy in my work, my horses were tamed by love and kindness, and I believe that the natives themselves on this *estancia* were beginning to treat their own horses better. I found that the news had spread around the countryside that a woman broke horses there, and I used to get stared at rather strangely wherever I went.

It was not many months after the locust invasion that I began to feel ill—I lost my appetite and was constantly sick. I didn't pay much attention to this at first, but I soon began to lose weight at an alarming speed, and to feel very weak, so I arranged to have myself taken by road into the town to see a native doctor, who arranged for urine and blood tests to be made. The results showed I had a five percent glycosuria, and he diagnosed diabetes. This meant that I had to take insulin and to suffer the terrible business of jabbing the stuff into my leg twice a day. Sometimes I went almost into a coma as a result of it and had to take sugar to make myself better. To make a long story short, before very long I knew I was dying, and in a matter of a few weeks I became a living skeleton and practically blind, and the doctor said he could do nothing more for me.

As a result of all this, I think I must have become delirious, my one idea now being to go out into the pampas to die. I knew that there was an extremely wicked horse in the barn that had thrown some of the peons very badly, and I thought that if only that horse would kill me I should then suffer no more. So, one day, when everyone had gone out I got my saddle and bridle, and very, very slowly I went out to the barn where the horse was kept. No one saw me go, for even my old cook had left two days before on some unknown mission. I went up to the black horse and again very slowly and with much effort saddled him up. Jean whined plaintively in the meantime, as if she knew I was doing wrong. I then climbed up the side of the box and into the saddle, trembling like a leaf all the time with fatigue. The horse moved off obediently. I urged him on faster as best I could, but he would do no more than break into the gentlest of trots. He went wherever I willed, and if he'd been the gentlest of horses he could not have behaved more beautifully. In that moment I realized once again that animals are always right, and I knew that I had been wicked even to have hoped that this beautiful creature might kill me. Slowly I rode him home. I was completely exhausted and he bore me along slowly and more gently than I could ever have imagined. I could no longer guide him myself, but he knew where to go and he brought me safely home. As we reached the *estancia* I saw that everyone was in a tremendous flurry, looking for me everywhere, but I was able to say nothing in explanation as they helped me into the house.

That night my old cook returned. She had been to see the Indians where she used to live, for she thought they knew a cure for diabetes. She had brought with her the fresh growing twigs of the Sarandi Blanco tree, and was soon cutting them into small pieces about four inches long and infusing them in hot water. The result was a pale green liquid which she begged me to drink. I felt it could do no harm in the circumstances, so I drank it, and then fell into a deep sleep. Next morning she brought me another dose and begged me not to give myself any more insulin, for she said that this remedy would cure me by itself. I obeyed her, for I had little to lose, and I took a glass of this daily for a week, soon beginning to feel better, and to be able to manage all right without the insulin. In three weeks I was feeling quite a different person and I knew I was getting well. She now told me to take a glass of the potion only every other day, instead of every day, and still with no ill results. Every day I got better and six weeks later I decided to stop the treatment altogether. This seemed to have no ill effects whatever, and from that day to this I have had no return of the illness. This treatment depends on having the young shoots of the tree, for the old twigs have no effect. Later, I and other English people brought bundles of the twigs home for an old colonel who had had diabetes for forty-seven years: in three days he was able to give up his insulin, but had to continue drinking a glass of the infusion every day, which suggests that it cures diabetes in the early stages, but only replaces the insulin in cases of long standing. But how much pleasanter the potion than jabbing a needle into oneself all the time!

Another drug commonly used in the Argentine and not found in England is Esculeol, a liquid of which forty drops are taken every day for not more than ten days, which is a wonderful cure for piles and varicose veins. I intend one day to get some more of it over here to find out exactly what it is.

I was persuaded to go back to England now that I was stronger, for fear that anything should go wrong again. So I had to pack up, meaning to return later on to my beloved dog and my horses. I hated the thought of leaving them all, although I knew my old cook would love Jean like a child. One day I had gone to speak to them in their room, and I found the two maids lying asleep on the floor and Jean in their bed with her head on the pillow. When I asked them what on earth they were doing, they said the floor was too hard for "poor Jean"!

The last weeks before I left for England were hell. Jean knew I was going away and used to lie with her head on my suitcase, her pitiful eyes begging for comfort. There were only two courses that I could take. One was to put her to sleep then and there, the other to leave her with Maria until my return, for I never thought then that I would never return. Years later, I discovered from a man who came on leave from the same *estancia* that the manager had never put Jean to sleep as I had asked, so my mind was tortured for twenty years until I heard the end of the story. My grandson went to a prep school in Entre Rios, and there was another English boy there who told my grandson about a Great Dane his father had owned named Jean. These people had adopted her, and she lived to the ripe old age of thirteen and a half. I'm glad these people were more devoted than that manager, whom Jean had hated on sight. I ought never have trusted him to carry out my wishes, though things turned out for the best. What a small world it is!

# *Marriage and War Years*

I spent four years in Argentina. On my return to England, I horse-dealt and it was through a former undergraduate friend of mine, Dr Felix Ingham, whom I knew before I went to the Argentine, that I met my husband, in a pub! As neither of us drinks, it was an unusual place for us to meet. Felix, having heard that I had some horses (as I had done before I left), used to turn up at Sandfield and help me exercise them. It was purely a platonic friendship. One evening, he suggested we meet at the George public house and then go on to Bampton Fair, some distance away. I was there at six o'clock, the appointed time, and he was late so I said to the barmaid, "Tell Dr Ingham that I wait for no man," and was actually going out of the door when he and another doctor, whom he introduced as Michael Woodhouse, came in, and we all went to Bampton Fair. Few will believe me when I tell them that love at first sight is definitely possible. I fell head over heels in love with Michael.

I was at that time running dances on Saturday evenings at Sandfield and inviting all my girlfriends to meet the young doctors from the Radcliffe Infirmary. Michael came to the next one and I am afraid, instead of being a good hostess and introducing everyone to each other as usual, I was out in the garden with Michael. Every evening we strolled by the river and the weather that summer stayed gloriously hot and dry for a very long time. Rumours of war brought us even closer together in the fear that, if war broke out, we might be separated. Six weeks after meeting we were engaged, much to the apparent annoyance of the other young doctors, who could see their Saturday evening dances dwindling into nothing. One remarked, "Engaged to Michael. Who is going to run the dances now?" As the phony war broke out, I took a job as a sort of personal assistant, secretary/help to one of the consultants at the Radcliffe and saw Michael quite often, as he was in the gynecological department under Professor Stalworthy and I was quite close by. We married the following August and our wedding must have been one of the most extraordinary ones ever.

As I was dressing to go to the church where my brother was to give me away, I suddenly got the most terrible cramp in my stomach. I could not stand up at all. Mother hastily telephoned Michael at the hospital and he came up and gave me some morphine, which temporarily stopped the pain but made my mouth so dry I could hardly speak. Charlie, my brother, had to go to church with a small bottle of water under his coat with which to wet my lips should I not be able to speak very easily. The service went off all right but the pain started to return after we got back for the reception, so we told our guests that we had to get away on our honeymoon, quickly changed, got into the car and drove just around the corner where we stayed until we thought everyone had gone away. I was in agony by then so we went back to Sandfield and I went to bed. Three days later we started our honeymoon in the Speech House Hotel in Gloucestershire; the bombs could be heard falling at infrequent intervals in the background.

During the war, my husband was unfit for military service and so was not called up, and we found ourselves in general practice in a small country town in Wiltshire. Life in this little manufacturing but countrified town was very different from anything I had ever led before. As wife of one of the local doctors I came under the criticism of everyone, and the people who lived there didn't take kindly to newcomers. I had always been a most friendly person, and I was staggered by the way people spoke to us. In the fish shop one morning an old boy said something about his wishing newcomers would stay away, a remark obviously directed at me, so I turned to him and asked him why he was so rude when he didn't even know me. His reply was, "We always treat foreigners with suspicion 'til we gets to know 'em." I assured him I was English, but he said, "You'm a foreigner jus' the same," and shuffled out. I gathered that it takes at least four years to be accepted as one of themselves.

I found life there rather slow at first and irritating. The perpetual phone calls interrupted my cooking or reading, and people so often seemed to wait until nine or ten o'clock at night before calling my husband out. It seemed unreasonable to me that after a heavy day's work he should have to start all over again, and few nights passed without his having to go out at some time or other. Mostly the calls proved quite unnecessary, but my husband assured me that when night falls people lose their nerve and feel that morning is so far away and that perhaps they should have called in the doctor. He always seemed so placid about everything, but I worried dreadfully over him, for at one time he had had lung trouble. I found the rude way some people rang up and said, "Send the doctor," instead of "Would the doctor please call," or some other polite message, very unpleasant. But I tried hard to remember that they were worried people, for I know so well that we can all be rude and abrupt when we are worried.

But I had many contacts with extremely nice people, and I was deeply touched by the troubles of some of the patients who used to come to call on my husband. Then they would find me sympathetic, and out would come all their worries. I found that if I just listened and let them talk, with just an occasional word of encouragement, it did more good than all the aspirins and brown-coloured medicines that we could produce. I remember once, when my husband was ill and the other doctors in the practice were very busy, I decided to go over to the surgery and run a shuttle service between my husband and the patients for the routine things like renewed prescriptions, only sending over to the other surgery cases that really needed the personal attention of a doctor. One dear old boy turned up and sat down and I asked him what was wrong. He said, "Nothing new," and that he had just come for a chat with the doctor, but that I'd do instead. So we chatted and I heard his troubles, which were actually more concerned I think with his pigs than with himself. He seemed quite satisfied, and when he next came he told my husband, "Mrs. Woodhouse did me a power of good and I be a mind I'll come and see her again" —bless him, for words such as those make life happier all around.

And so while the war dragged on, Michael and I lived and worked in Wiltshire, he seeing patients and I working for the local War Agricultural Committee and giving birth to our three children, Pamela, Judith and Patrick. When the war ended, and we were free to move at last, we found a larger farm within reasonable reach of London, where my husband would be studying for another three years. We lived on this farm until Michael finished his examinations and found a post in London, where he would remain for twenty-six years. As he found the long train journey into the city each day tiring, we looked for a place nearer London —a difficult task, as we soon discovered, for we had to have land and sheds for my cows. But at long last, we found a large house in Croxley Green with ten acres and stables to go with it. I could now begin some of the projects I had in mind.

# Jyntee

After the war when we moved to Campions, our home at Croxley Green, I wanted another Dane. Having been deprived of a dog for so long under war conditions I felt now we had a big house and garden that once again I could own a dog. I saw an advertisement for some Dane puppies near London and went off to see them. They were the most dreadful, skinny, sick-looking puppies I'd ever seen, but their mother and I just fell in love with each other on sight. She had big beautiful eyes and was a fawn with a black mask. She put her nose into my hand and asked as plainly as if she had spoken the words to come with me; it was only then I noticed that she only had half a tail. Apparently, that is how the owner came to have her. The breeder found the dam had bitten off some of Jyntee's tail at birth and she was useless for show purposes so was sold to the present owners, who bred with her. I asked if

I could have her instead of a puppy, and the owner looked most surprised and replied that they'd had her six years and they were sure she wouldn't go with me. So I asked them if I went to my car and opened the back door and Jyntee came with me of her own free will, could I buy her? The answer was yes, confident she would not go with me. I called Jyntee from the car, she raced to it and jumped in and lay down; she was mine. Patrick and Judith were thrilled when I arrived home with her and Jyntee just fitted in at once.

I noticed that the following Saturday, two days after I got her, there was to be a charity fête locally and one of the events was to be a comic dog show. One class was for the dog with the most tricks, and the children begged me to teach Jyntee some tricks so she could go in for that class. Jyntee was quite amazing; she learned eleven different tricks in two days, including rolling over, jumping through a hoop, picking her name out of the alphabet, counting by barking on my signal, finding my article among others of the same sort put down by other people, and of course easily won the competition. She so enjoyed being applauded. I think all dogs love being applauded. It is routine in my training school when a dog has done right.

Jyntee learned that cows have horns and can butt rather hard if you get the wrong end of them. She used to help in everything we did on the farm, bringing the calves their milk, bringing in the cows, riding with me when I was schooling ponies, and playing endlessly with the children. They would go and hide and she

*Jyntee*

would pretend she couldn't find them, then suddenly
pretend she'd seen them and bound up with a bark.
She always lay on the bottom of the stairs in the hall,
looking so beautiful. I don't think anyone ever noticed
her broken tail. I wrote my first book for my children,
which was called *Jyntee, The Tale of a Dog with a Broken
Tail,* so many other children shared Jyntee's adventures when it was published (a task which I undertook
myself with great difficulty but determination).

All my life I seem to have had bad luck with the
animals I love so dearly. Jyntee began to go lame on
a back leg and bone cancer was diagnosed. I kept her
six months after this, but when I saw that the bone was
so fragile that the leg would soon break I made the
heartbreaking decision to put her to sleep. My only
comfort was that her short life with us had been a very
happy one. Before she went I bought Juno, a very
nervous puppy who later became known worldwide,
and who was in my eyes one of the most wonderful
dogs ever born.

137

# Juno

Juno came to me only because the Dane puppy I had bought from a very big breeder who was giving up Danes arrived with a temperature of 105°F. I rang the breeder and told her the puppy was not well and I wasn't going to keep her. I'd just lost my Jyntee and couldn't face another ill dog. So she said she hadn't got another puppy suitable for me; all she had was a brindle bitch of three months who was terribly nervous, so I said I didn't mind nerves, I was sure I could cure those, but I didn't want an ill dog. We arranged to meet at Oxford halfway between the breeder's home and mine and exchange puppies. I arrived before the breeder did, and was horrified to see her open her car trunk, inside which was this nervous puppy. I took one look at her and I knew she must be mine. No one who loved dogs could let her continue her life in this state of terror. So we swapped the very beautiful sick fawn puppy for the brindle who was to become my Juno.

I wonder what these hereditary nerves come from. Other Danes on the breeder's premises were healthy and didn't look nervous. The fawn puppy was not nervous; why should just one be like this?

If you touched Juno from the back and she didn't see you going to do it, she screamed with continuing yells as if she had been run over. She was rickety but otherwise healthy. I immediately started training her to walk on a loose lead in the town, Woolworth's being my main training area. A nervous dog must walk on a loose lead among legs and people, shopping baskets, sticky-fingered children who try to pat her and all the rest of the obstacles one encounters in a town. She got quite firm jerks on her choke chain if she sat back. If people touched her she screamed at first, which gave the people an awful shock and, I hope, taught them to leave other people's dog's alone. Bit by bit she stopped screaming and began to enjoy her walks in town. I taught her to sit and stay while I did my shopping, first of all in the shop where I could watch her reactions to crowds and to people bending to pat her, which she soon ignored. Her fear quickly vanished and a confident ignoring of other people made her safe to leave sitting whatever the distractions that occurred.

I then started really obedience training her. Having watched an obedience competition at an agricultural show, I felt certain that Juno could do all those things quite easily. But I realized I should probably join a dog training club to learn all the ins and outs of show obedience, something I had never done. So by the time Juno was six months old she was confident, happy, longing to learn and a glorious dog to look at, with terrific bone structure, her only two faults being her flying ears and rather thick underneck. As neither these faults nor any others she may have had from the show point of view mattered for the obedience ring, I felt that should be her initial training.

I took her over to a dog training club and asked if I could join with Juno. They said, "No, no Dane could be obedience trained," so I asked if I could watch that evening's work and I was allowed to. When they came to the advanced work for Test C there were only a few dogs in that class, so I asked if Juno could try one or two of the exercises; I was permitted to try. Juno did them reasonably well and I felt confident I could train her in this work.

I found another club which held its meetings on Sunday mornings at the Master Robert pub at Hounslow called the West Middlesex, and there I was received with great warmth. The trainers there were quite wonderful, and Juno and I advanced our knowledge in no time at all. Then came the chance of a lifetime for me. The West Middlesex was to challenge the club that had refused me to a match, and we all drew lots for who should represent our club in each obedience test. Juno and I drew Test C, the most difficult test in obedience, and as luck would have it, I was drawn against the trainer of that club who had refused me as a member, and it was just a few weeks since I'd

joined the West Middlesex and started training Juno in
competitive obedience. I know it's boasting but I hope
it gives courage to the weak to know that Juno beat the
other trainer's Alsatian in the match to win Test C.
May this be a lesson to all trainers not to say any dog
is untrainable until they have seen whether it is the dog
or its owner who needs the instruction most. I have
proved time and time again that it is the owners who
need much more training than the dogs. So many owners are terribly dull; their dogs hate working for this
reason. Boredom is death to happy work. You need to
be outgoing to get the best from any dog, but this does
not mean noisy and blustering. I think training clubs
could leave the dogs out of the first few lessons and
teach owners voice control, signals, and how to be
enthusiastic, for to succeed in obedience the dogs must
be happy.

# Getting into
# Show Business

People have often said to me, "How did you start getting your Juno known and into films and television?" This is a long story. The first thing I did was of course to obedience train her. She was one of the first Danes to take part in public obedience competitions, and she always attracted a lot of attention, especially as we also had Chica, the tiny little black-and-tan terrier, as the breed was then known, with Juno. This tiny mite would sit between Juno's paws and of course that was just what made a picture for the press. Without the press, practically nothing can be achieved. I was lucky enough to meet dozens of charming people from the press in conjunction with my next book, *Talking to Animals,* when I appeared many times on television with Juno and spoke on the radio, and I was happy to get a lot of press publicity. It was always Juno who posed for the pictures that were original and were well received by the national newspapers, so the photographers were delighted and used to ring me up and ask me to do some sessions at my home for the magazines and papers. I have literally hundreds and hundreds of photos of my dogs doing just everything. I have ten huge volumes of press cuttings so I shall never really be without my dogs. I only have to open these books and be lost in the world of my Danes.

The next thing I did was road safety. I trained Juno to look both ways before crossing the road and not to cross if there was anything coming. I taught her never to fetch a ball if it ran into the road. I taught her to drop down on signal at a great distance to prevent her ever running into the road by mistake even if she was in the country, although I do not advocate any dog's being off the lead where there is traffic, however well trained it is. Then I started approaching the road safety officers in districts within reasonable distance of me, and offered to give road safety training demonstrations for dogs, and talks if they would organize the hall. I borrowed a film on dogs and road safety from the Royal Society for the Prevention of Accidents, and at the end of the talk invited anyone with a dog to let me show them how easy it was to teach it to behave. Slowly I graduated to doing Saturday morning children's cinema matinee performances. In the intermission I would take my dogs and draw a white line on the stage and ask the children to shout whether there was a car coming or not. If they yelled yes Juno would not go across the line. If they said no she crossed. The same when we threw an object: if the children said traffic was coming Juno never retrieved it; if the road was clear she would go across and fetch it on command, never without command. The children loved the dogs Juno and Chica and the requests for these demonstrations and talks grew and grew. More press write-ups came our way.

Then I decided to start a dog-training class at Croxley Green. I put an advertisement in the local paper asking people to contact me if they would like a dog-training club to be set up with me as trainer. Six people answered and the Croxley Canine Training Club came into being. The only hut we could get on a Sunday morning was the Territorial building at Croxley where the guns were stored, but it was dry and we could do heel work in the rather confined area around the guns. Juno always demonstrated the correct obedience, and I taught these six people. Soon we were overflowing with requests for training and to make a long story short, I was soon running six clubs in different districts. Every night I ran one within a radius of about ten miles and on Sunday I ran one at my home. Sometimes there were as many as sixty dogs in a class. I used to charge a shilling a lesson to pay for the halls I had to hire in other districts. But mothers and fathers got cunning and I discovered children were borrowing neighbours' dogs and being sent up to me on a Sunday afternoon so that Mum and Dad could put their feet up and let me cope with the children! This was not a good thing as the dogs they borrowed neither loved them nor obeyed them at all and I put a stop to it. Over seven thousand dogs passed through my hands when I was running dog clubs, and Juno was always the dog that showed people how to train their dogs if a demonstration was needed. This led to her being asked to appear at fêtes and give a show of her tricks etc.; I was delighted to do this.

Perhaps one of the most amusing things I organized for Juno's publicity to help the Guide Dogs for the Blind was to ask permission to collect at the Championship Cat Show at Olympia one year. Some of the cat owners weren't all that pleased at a dog being at the show, but most of them knowing how gentle Juno was were delighted at the television and national newspaper publicity. Juno was put into a cage of baby kittens and adored them. She always had a very motherly attitude to other animals, and when the champion cat was chosen for the supreme prize it lay between Juno's great paws for innumerable photographs to be taken by the press. We raised quite a considerable amount in Juno's boxes for the Guide Dogs for the Blind. Neither Juno nor my next dog, ever chased cats; I think they understood that here in our home anything like that was just not on, as our cat understood that to kill a bird was a crime in our eyes. Birds built their nests at our front door and baby birds flopped about all over the place but neither cat nor Dane would injure them in any way. Words were enough to teach the two dogs what I wanted, but one good smack taught the cat the only time she caught a bird. I never had to smack my

dogs, although I am not one of those sentimental people who say a dog should never be smacked. If I
thought a dog warranted that sort of punishment I
would do it without regret of any sort. It often shortens
the time spent in training when the dog is really doing
wrong and not listening to words of reprimand. This
doesn't happen if the dog is trained from its earliest
days.

I once had to take Juno for a television taping where
there were six cats in the same scene. All the cats were
in the kitchen. Juno was to rush in and all the cats were
supposed to jump up into different places. This seemed
impossible; in the end I practiced each cat separately
and it was achieved, but cats are not easy to work like
dogs; food is the best way to get them to do things.

I always remember Juno collecting for the blind at
the United Charities Bazaar in the Watford Town
Hall. She was a dog who would wag her tail at everyone in the hope they would put money in her boxes.
She knew as well as I did that this was something she
was supposed to do. One man came up to her and
spoke to her and she lifted her upper lip in a warning
growl, something I had never seen her do in her life.
I told the man to leave her alone and went to the
policeman at the Town Hall entrance and asked him
to keep an eye on this man. A short time after the man
was arrested for shoplifting. How can a dog sum up
character like this and warn me of danger ahead?

I remember one experience with Juno which had
extraordinary results. I had left my car in Piccadilly

before the age of traffic wardens and on returning to it, some two hundred yards away I saw a man with a key trying to open the door. Juno was police-work trained, so I let her off the lead and gave her the command to "get him," which she swiftly did. I arrested the man and handed him to a police officer, but afterwards I got a letter from Scotland Yard telling me they would overlook this instance but I must not put my dog on one of Her Majesty's subjects or I would be liable to prosecution, not being a member of the police force (even though I trained one of the first Alsatians ever to be accepted by the police in the 1920s and later trained the demonstration Alsatian team belonging to the Thames Valley Police). After this I saw a bank raid at the White City and as I had Juno with me, I could easily have freed her and possibly have caught one of the thieves, but this time I just watched the escape. What a silly law if you are to let your property be stolen and own a dog who could stop it.

My dogs were trained never to bite. The chases they have done in films were always done with actors without padding, for I had trained my Danes only to slip their teeth onto the clothing of the arm, not the flesh.

This is how I think dogs should be trained to guard the home. Bark and cease barking on command, attack if given the command, and sit instantly the attacked person stands still without threatening anyone. At the slightest move hold him until he stands still again, have no fear of gunfire, and remain a friendly dog to all until told not to be friendly. The ordinary owner would need years of experience to teach a Dane all this, but it is fun trying.

If film and television people know of a well-trained dog and the property master of the big companies is informed, there may one day be a chance for your Dane to appear in the movies. You will never be told what to do until they want to film you, you will be treated like the "property" you are, the hours will be long, the nervous tension killing, but the pleasure of watching your dog will compensate for all this. Occasionally you watch and your dog doesn't appear, you have told all your friends to watch, you've spent a fortune on phoning all and sundry to watch or go to the movies and your dog is not seen. The cruelty of the scissors on the cutting room floor is quite unbelievable; it's happened to all of us—but carry on, one day your dog may be a star like mine were.

People always ask how dog food commercials are done and whether the dog always eats the food or likes the food it advertises, and I always quote what happened with a famous actor doing a beer commercial in which I was involved. He was a teetotaller and nothing would make him drink beer, so Coca-Cola was drunk instead. My dog was supposed to drink a glass of beer too: even if I had allowed such a thing, I am sure she wouldn't have liked beer. I certainly would not have any dog of mine doing such an unnatural thing, so she had red gravy to drink.

Once again, for this commercial I was called in to do it at the last moment by a desperate producer who rang me and asked me to get in my car and rush up to London instantly, as they'd been trying for over two hours to get the shot, and the Afghan chosen to do the commercial wouldn't do a thing. I rushed up and Juno was bundled out of the car, rushed into the pub where the action was to take place, shown what the action was to be (which was to jump with her forefeet onto the counter and be given half a pint of "beer" and drink it with the actor drinking his pint at the same time). She did it immediately and I noticed the sweat running off everyone's brow, and I wondered why they were all so het up. I wasn't worried at all. After being paid a miserable six pounds for Juno's efforts, someone said to me, "You silly fool, you should have charged them fifty pounds." The actor was getting a thousand pounds, and another a thousand pounds if the performance wasn't completed by twelve o'clock midday. It was eleven fifty-five when Juno completed the scene.

Dog food commercials are sometimes a hazard when the camera or actors or clients have difficulties, for no dog can go on eating and eating and eating food however much it likes it. On the outside of most tins is given the right amount for a dog of a certain size for a day. If this is exceeded the dog may get an upset stomach, as anyone might who overeats. The food in front of the dish has to be made easier to film by being occasionally coloured and sometimes having glycerine over it to make it shine. This is ordinary advertising technique, so the dog mostly eats from the back of the dish if this is done. If the food has to be eaten more times than is good for the dog, due to technical hitches, one of course has to use something else which would not upset the dog. There is a limit to any dog's appetite so it is usual to take more than one dog of the same breed to the studio. With my Danes this was impossible—everyone knew them from their films and television appearances so I always nagged the production manager to get the camera crew right on their toes and make certain their side of the work didn't let my dog down. In most cases although my dog and I were booked for a day's work it was finished in about two hours. Being Danes they could eat quite a lot anyway!

# Climbing the Ladder to Success

On reading this book people may imagine that the making of my dogs into film stars was something quite easy. Actually it was slavery. England is not the land of Rin Tin Tins or Lassies; people mostly think of dogs merely as companions, playthings for the children or show dogs, as well as guards of their property. There must be few people who know the joy I have experienced in training my dogs to almost human intelligence and understanding. I am sure there are many people who own the most intelligent dogs, whom they adore and who adore them in return, but I wonder if those dogs would show all that intelligence when asked to act with complete strangers, in strange surroundings, maybe with actors who don't even like dogs and who are only doing their work for a fee. These were the problems I had to cope with even after I got recognition that my dogs would act with anyone.

The first film I did was for the Children's Film Foundation after being introduced to the boss of a small film company in Dean Street, Soho. He was fascinated by Juno's size and somehow managed to interest Mary Field, who was the head of the Children's Film Foundation in this country. She came down to my home to talk to me and be introduced to Juno. The result was the film company wrote a suitable script called *Juno Helps Out* and planned it to be performed by my two children Judith, aged eight, and Patrick, aged six, neither of whom had ever acted before, with of course Juno as the star.

The company, prior to making the film, came and made one scene here as a tryout and it was approved, so shooting started. Our home was turned into a film studio. Great cables passed through our windows and we had to put up with draughts everywhere. The children were worked terribly hard and once Patrick was reduced to tears, which made me angry, but the results were lovely and eventually the film made its first appearance at a big cinema in London on a Saturday morning with an invited audience. Juno went onstage after the showing to get the applause of the gathering, and she was launched as the Lassie of England. The film was taken everywhere with Mary Field, as an example of what should be made for children, and took an award at the Venice Festival as the best children's film of the year. It ran on the matinees for years and years, and I believe is still doing so.

Alas, that was not the commencement of work for

Juno as I'd hoped. People still didn't cotton on to the value of a dog to bring in the crowds to the cinemas and I got tired of waiting for the phone to ring with big offers.

One day I was working at Pinewood on *Appointment with Venus,* which was the story of a cow, not a dog, and as usual I only went to the studios if my Juno was allowed to accompany me, even though she was not being employed in any way. She always lay on the set watching everything. It was a good training for her future in films to get used to the banging of carpenters, the tension when the words "All quiet, roll it" were shouted out and the atmosphere that she must have picked up when everyone was on edge.

In between scenes I got talking to the chief cameraman, who said the film business was doing poorly and after this film he would be without work. My brain suddenly functioned. I asked him if he'd like to make films for me with Juno and my children. He said he would very much, and that is how I went home to write scripts for six thirty-minute films to be shot on sixteen millimeters in black and white. I only wrote outline scripts without actual dialogue because we couldn't afford direct sound. I could only afford to put on a commentary afterwards, so the films had to be so self-explanatory that actual words were of no great importance.

Shortly after the films were made I took Juno to a few movie studio property masters. Property masters are the powers that be who book dogs, which are property as far as films are concerned, unless they are starring in something, when they become actors. The property masters were most impressed with Juno when shown a few things she could do, and whenever there was a chance for her to appear in a film they booked her.

Directors found Juno easy to work with. I can't ever remember being given a shooting script before the dog was actually asked to act, which always amazed me. They all concluded Juno would do the things they asked for. Woe betide me if I ever dared to ask where the dog's entrance would be or exactly what she was supposed to do until just before shooting. I would be brushed aside with an annoyed look implying that I was a nuisance to say the least.

Juno soon was in tremendous demand. She appeared in films and shows with stars like Alec Guinness, Peter Finch and Adrienne Corri in *Make Me an Offer*, series like the *Invisible Man, The International Detective, The Avengers, Robin Hood, Lancelot,* etc. and with individual stars like David Frost, Roger Moore, and others. None of the actors or actresses she ever performed with appeared jealous or afraid of her stealing the picture, rather they took the view that more people would probably pay to see the film if a dog appeared and certainly the *Radio Times* and *T.V. Times* used to give her a credit, which I am sure made more people watch the program.

Juno was by this point leading the life of a human

film star, fetched to the studios in a Rolls-Royce, star on her dressing-room door, written up and used by publicity departments in practically everything she appeared in. Then came the great offer of half a million pounds for her to go to the States and star in a series of sixty-nine television episodes of a series to be written for her. This I could not accept; with quarantine regulations, my beloved dog would be utterly miserable if she had to leave me. Money meant nothing where my dogs were concerned. The fun of working her in films or television was all the reward I wanted. It was a great disappointment not to be able to accept, nor to be able to persuade the company to come to England to do the series.

I think the biggest disappointment of all was when Juno went on location to Cornwall, with Clark Gable for the film *Never Let Me Go,* and the abominable weather only made it possible to shoot two scenes before the company had to return to Boreham Wood and do the scenes in a boat on an artificial lake, rather than on the sea which it was scheduled to do. The producer did not feel Juno could act in a small boat on a lake safely and her part landed up on the cutting-room floor. In any case making this film with Juno was not a happy experience, as every time Clark Gable forgot his part, some of which had to be written up on a blackboard and held over his head while he spoke the lines, he told the director Juno made him forget his lines. This really annoyed me as Juno did everything she was told as always, never fluffing anything, which was more than I can say for some of the humans she performed with in her life.

Juno's life with me must have been one of the busiest any dog ever knew. I never left her for the first nine years of my life with her; wherever I went she went. No invitation was accepted unless she was invited too. In fact as the years with her went by people got to asking Juno to things rather than me, knowing full well that would bring me along too. Or so I hope!

# Goodbye, Juno

I suppose I should call myself lucky to have had Juno for eleven and a half years. Danes usually have short lives. She was in superb form all her life. She never went as grey on the face as some Danes do, and I doubt if anyone seeing her working would have known she was over eleven years old. Alas, tragedy was to take her from me.

I got a call from television to take my dogs, Juno and little Chica her pal, as well as three other dogs to be collected from people who'd trained these dogs in my school, and go to St. Martin's Theatre, London, for filming. I was not told what the dogs had to do but this was not unusual. I got my assistant, Anne West, to come with me. The dogs all behaved perfectly in the train and we got out at Finchley Road station to change trains. There was a train standing with open doors at the opposite platform. I got Chica in and was getting

Juno in when without any warning from anyone the doors closed on Juno's tummy, and the train went off with her firmly fixed in the door. Another passenger and I struggled to open the doors but nothing would do this. Never believe that tube trains can't go off without the doors being properly shut. Anne was left behind on the platform with the three dogs. When the train stopped at the next station the doors opened and Juno was freed. She was panting a bit, but I felt that she would best forget this incident if she did some work, as she didn't seem hurt. I returned to Finchley Road station and picked up Anne and the dogs and continued with our journey. When we got there Anne recognized Jonathan Routh and said "Candid Camera," and we realized this filming was to be just one of the episodes used in that program and came home immediately.

That night Juno didn't seem well. Her heart started pounding a lot. Next day I left her at home with my help while I went shopping and on my return the help opened the front door and Juno rushed out to greet me. Before I could kiss her she dropped dead at my feet. People tried to comfort me by telling me how nice it was that she didn't suffer long, nor really grow old, that she'd worked almost up to her death, but I'd lost one of my family, not just a dog. The newspapers wrote up her tragic end, and letters poured in from all over the world.

Juno lies buried in my garden, one of the most precious friends I've ever owned.

# The New Arrival

After Juno died my husband begged me to get another dog quickly. I didn't feel like doing this at all. I was devastated, but he was right, and when Mrs. Davies of the Oldmanor Danes offered me a bitch puppy out of a litter she had with two brindles in it, I went up to see them. The moment I set eyes on the bold puppy that came out to greet me I knew she must be mine. Both her parents were champions and she had the deep golden undercoat and tiger markings that I so love. She was just six weeks old. She came in the car with me lying contentedly on a rug on the seat and slept most of the way home.

Junia I called her. I couldn't use the name Juno again; it was sacred to that lovely dog now gone. I had to choose a name that meant something and this surely did. I always shortened it to Juni because the *i* at the end made it easy for the puppy to identify herself with that name. Junia would have had one syllable too many for quick communication. And Junia, if I had anything to do with it and had any luck at all, would follow in Juno's footsteps as nearly as I could train her to do so. But the extraordinary thing was she somehow seemed to know what to do. I only had to show her once and she instantly did the thing that would normally take a puppy some weeks to learn. I had a feeling my Juno had come back to me inside this amazing puppy.

Chica, our little black-and-tan terrier, took to her at once and played endlessly with her, although she herself was nearly twelve years old, and I have the joy of having all these early days of Junia and Chica in a film called *A Star Is Made.* This had cinema showing, and lots of sixteen-millimeter copies have gone out all over the world. No one can deny that lovely intelligent look on Junia's face, or the way she does the tricks which Juno did and which she performed for this film so naturally that anyone seeing it would imagine all the actions were as Junia thought them up. Junia was different in character from Juno. Juno was always a placid dog; Junia was always wanting to do things, her ability to learn and do was unending.

When Junia was four months old M.G.M. rang me and said they wanted a Dane for their new film. Did I have one? I looked at Junia and asked them if I could bring her to see them, as although she was only four months old they didn't want a dog for another five weeks, and knowing how Danes grow, I felt Junia might by then be big enough. I knew I could train her

to do anything I wanted, or rather *they* wanted, because she already knew so many things, including an
attack on a supposed criminal, and she was completely
unafraid of gunfire. Her brain was so big the sky was
the limit.

The production manager and the director looked at
her and at once said, "Yes, providing she grows
enough," so that was that. Junia ate everything, her
rate of growth was tremendous; so at the appointed
date we took her to M.G.M. to be seen, and the contract was ours. The coincidence was that Juno's first
feature film assignment was with Clark Gable for
M.G.M., and now Junia's first feature film was to be for
M.G.M., too. I felt she was to follow exactly in Juno's
footsteps. The film was a great success.

Junia's fame spread quickly. She was soon appearing
on television shows and getting attention in the press
and even on the radio. She also did commercials for
masses of different products, from the Gas Council to
the selling of cars, horse feed and cookers. She appeared at multiple stores, lectures, fêtes, schools, etc.,
besides all her work in films and television. Sometimes
the fees she got were in keeping with her star status;
at other times she worked for a pittance for a small film
company with a tiny budget. Money never really bothered me; it was the fun of achieving something and
being so proud of Junia that I worked for.

Always my mind was on one big thing and one big
thing only. I wanted to star Junia in a big colour film.
It looked as if this ambition would never be achieved,

so in a case like this there is only one thing to do: do
it oneself. I sat down and wrote a script about a miner's
son who wanted to become a pop star, and who, on
hitchhiking to London, stopped for the night at a farm.
There he met a Great Dane who had been taken in by
the farmer's wife when found wandering on the farm,
obviously abandoned by a motorist going on holiday.
The adventures of this boy and the dog and the boy's
hopes and disappointments in his efforts to become a
pop star were the plot of the story. I tried to get profes-
sional scriptwriters to help me put my outline in order,
but I was too small-fry. Either they simply replied they
didn't do other people's script ideas, or they weren't
interested. But I persisted and finally found a cooperative crew and cast. The film was called *Along the Way*
and actually did pretty well. But I don't think I will
make another film on my own—there is too much
worrying and risk. I do feel, however, that I learned
a good deal from the experience.

# Action!

I hope people reading this book won't think I exploited my dogs in show business. The training of them was the greatest joy to me and to them. Nobody who ever met my dogs or worked with them could doubt that to work with a loved mistress and to receive the praise and adoration they received from all and sundry must be a happy life for any dog.

The teaching of the actions that the dogs would need in their work was purely a matter of finding what made them do things. For example, I found it difficult to teach Junia to howl. She would whine but didn't catch on that that was not enough. Howling shows unhappiness and Junia was never unhappy. Then luck came my way and a jack donkey was put in my neighbour's field. He brayed incessantly and Junia hated this noise and set up a big howl of irritation. This was my chance. Every time she howled I said, "Howly," and

she soon knew what to do. My tone of voice when
giving her that command was almost a howl too. Tone
of voice matters terribly: the excited tone for a chase,
a tired tone for a yawn, a curious tone when she had
to dig up the ground and a sleepy tone for when she
had to shut her eyes and feign sleep on command.

It is terribly tiring teaching a dog new things, not
only for it but for me. Great concentration is necessary
and instant change of mood when the dog is succeed-
ing in doing what I want. Dogs who are not really as
one with their owners or handlers are unlikely to learn
quickly. A tremendous bond has to exist between
them. If one is upset it is useless trying to teach a dog
anything; if one is frightened for any reason that fear
will communicate itself to the dog by scent. Worrying
over something also communicates itself to a dog. So,
in fact, dog training, especially in show business, is not
all honey. One of the most difficult things to cope with
is the admiration the dog gets on the studio floor.
Everyone wants to talk to her or pat her and this tires
the dog. Yet the atmosphere on the set is good for the
dog. If she is put into a dressing room she just relaxes
and goes to sleep and it takes a good run in the open
air to wake her up. Sometimes the director will change
the action the dog has to do in the middle. It may be
she has to make an entrance from a different side. This
may muddle the dog and the best thing to do is to take
her out for a run for a few minutes and start again as
if it were a new action.

Juno and Junia had brains that were so big that they

could pick up any new thing in a few minutes. Junia
even reasoned out things for herself which helped the
film. In one film she was acting with a child who was
coming down a ladder. Junia was waiting at the bottom
and as the child came within reaching distance of her
head she licked the child's legs, which much improved
the scene, but was entirely her own idea. At home one
day my husband saw her trying to bring both her feeding bowl and our little terrier Mini's at the same time,
which of course was impossible. Then he saw her,
entirely unaided, think the problem out. She put the
two bowls inside each other and could then lift them
up. After that we wondered what would happen if we
put two bowls for her to bring which would not fit
inside each other. This took her a very short time to
solve. She put the two edges together and brought
them to us. This I have on film. Junia seemed to pick
up the thread of the story that was being filmed in an
almost human way and lots of times her expression has
added to the finished film. I suppose living so much
with me and my family, with all that went on here,
helped to make her that way. She and I were never
parted for a single day in her whole life.

# $\mathcal{My}$ $\mathcal{Family}$

My husband and I have been married for over forty years and have been exceptionally lucky. Except for one short stay in hospital, we have rarely been separated since the day we were married. Our likes and dislikes are the same and we laugh at the same things. In fact, I really think my husband is rather long-suffering. I make a lot of jokes during the day, and some of them may not be funny at all, but he always laughs! We do not go to the theatre, we do not drink and we do not smoke. In fact, people must think our life style extraordinarily dull. But, of course, we do not think that—we are perfectly happy in each other's company. When we married, people said that we looked alike, we might have been brother and sister. Well, we are alike in ourselves now and had no need to celebrate our ruby wedding anniversary in August 1980 as every day has been a celebration.

My husband loves animals. He has not got the gift I have, but I doubt if it would be good if we both had it. The three children, Pamela, Judith and Patrick, have also not got my gift with animals although they have been good with them most of their lives. When they were young, they spent a lot of time with cows, dogs and horses. My son, Patrick, when little, would go down to the field and ride my cows up to the yard without the slightest fear, and the bull used to watch the children having a dip in hot weather in the water tank in the yard. He was very gentle, until one day a boy put his dog over our fence and it attacked the bull. I had to go in and rescue the boy, who had stupidly climbed over the fence to get his dog. From that day on, my bull was not safe with people and had to be sold. When I returned the boy and his dog to his mother, instead of thanking me, she remarked that I looked more like a bull than the bull! I give up!

Chica was Judith's dog, whom she trained to go in for top obedience competition work. We used to go to obedience shows with our two dogs, my Juno and her tiny Chica. She often beat the German Shepherds. When she first started, Chica was only six months old and Judith six years old. The main problem then was people clapping. The sight of both of them working together brought thunderous applause and once, when Chica had just done a retrieve, the onlookers clapped so suddenly that the little dog got a fright and dropped the dumbbell, which I always thought was very bad luck for Judith. A watching crowd should learn to keep absolutely quiet until the end of an obedience test or the dog may well drop the dumbbell or do something silly. Judith also used to ride her pony with me in the early mornings when I would often ride one of my cows, but she was not as keen on horses as I was.

My eldest girl, Pamela, was always mad on horses and, in this respect of course, she followed in my footsteps. She went to a finishing school in Switzerland, at Château-d'Oex, where the headmistress also loved horses. When madame arrived in London for interviews with parents of prospective students she greeted us, holding in one hand a handbag with stirrup handles. She had a stirrup leather around her suit and we talked not about Pamela's education, but about how the children rode and the number of horses they had at the school. When I told her that Pamela had a favourite pony she said, "Well, why not send it out with Pamela to school?" I thought that would be lovely so I sent her pony, Freddie, out with her and it nearly broke us financially. The cost of sending the pony out to Switzerland and the forms to fill in, together with the dreadful job of getting him there, was very much more than we had bargained for. But I had promised Pamela that he would go with her and we kept our promise. She had a wonderful time at the school, with lessons well in second place to riding, although she did of course come back speaking fluent French. She rode against the Swiss Army in jumping competitions and beat them. When her two years out there came to an end, we found it impossible to bring her pony home

so we reluctantly gave him as a present to the school.
I hoped that future pupils would enjoy riding him for
he really was a lovely pony. Pamela used to spend
much of her free time when she was back riding in
competitions, going to pony camps and doing all the
things that the young girls today have a chance to do.

I wish my family had my gift with animals, for there
is a tremendous opening in training dogs, but there it
is. My little granddaughter, Harriet, however, has a
lovely way with dogs and, although she is only seven
now, I am hoping that when she grows up she may
carry on and help people with their dogs. She trains
her own little dog, Pica, who is a miniature pinscher,
and gives all the right signals in the right tone of voice,
and of course the dog obviously enjoys it. Perhaps the
gift has skipped a generation. There will not be another *Walkies with Woodhouse* but there may be a *Walkies with Harriet Walpole!*

# A Day in My Life

I think very few people of my age would survive the amount I have to do in a day. I sleep very badly as my mind will not stop working, so a lot of my planning takes place at night. I am always longing to get up at about four A.M. but have to keep quiet for the sake of the other members of the household. I think few people realize how glorious the scents and quiet of the countryside are at this time of the morning, but then you see I have been used for twenty years to milking my cows at five A.M., then taking my dog and pony out for about six miles before breakfast. When I was filming at the studios, which in the past took up a large proportion of my working week, the dog was often on call at about eight A.M. By then, she had had her exercise and was ready to do a hard day's work. I felt fit as a fiddle with all the fresh air I had had, whatever the weather, and the only boring thing was sitting doing nothing, perhaps all that day, in the studios. I found the repetitive rehearsals for the actors or actresses extremely dull and often felt I could have taught a dozen dogs by the time they had got their lines or actions right. I think the life of a human actor or actress must be quite dreadful. Even for a dog, the rehearsals and retakes kill the spontaneity that goes with "Take 1." When I am filming, as happened in the BBC series *Training Dogs the Woodhouse Way*, it is always the first take that is the best, with no rehearsals. Had I rehearsed them, the dogs would have been too good too soon and the idea of teaching the training would have been lost. In my second BBC special it was the same; everything had to be "Take 1" because you cannot breathe up an animal's nose twice, as it is a greeting between them and other animals or humans. I must be terrible to work with as I get so impatient with all the fiddling that seems necessary to set up the camera, just as the animal is waiting to do what I want. I am lucky in having been with a cooperative lighting camerman, on both the BBC series and the BBC special with animals. He soon learned how vital speed and mobility were in an animal series and never got offended at my urgent pleas to be quick. I think people realize how keen I am to get the absolute best out of not only animals but humans and soon pick up the atmosphere of urgency needed in this work.

Since January 1980, when my series *Training Dogs the Woodhouse Way* first came out, I have been inundated by the press for interviews, which I am delighted to give, but I hate being photographed. Instead of just, say, taking two photographs and going away, photographers seem to want as many pictures of me as they take of model girls, and slowly my smile wilts or my face grows stiff, not having been trained in the art of mastering the plastic face which can keep its expression for minutes on end. I suppose few people as old as I am like their wrinkles put onto paper. When I was young, except for a few snapshots on special occasions, I ran away from all photographers. The only photograph I really posed for was one which I sent to a casting agency when I felt I would like to be a cowgirl, in Western films, riding glorious horses out on the range. I got no replies so obviously I was not good enough, and now I am glad, with all my experience of making films, that I was not offered work.

One of the things that keeps me busy is my work as a publisher. My husband puts all the prices on the books, which means unwrapping them all, sticking labels on them and putting them back in the packets. I do all the invoices and the book work, and wrap them for posting. I think I could get a job in a dispatch department if I get too old to do anything else! Just because I run my businesses from home does not mean I work any less than any commuting family who leave home at 8:30 A.M. and return at 6:30 P.M. As well as my business side, I still have most of the household shopping to do. If I am filming or otherwise occupied, I plan meals a week ahead. I can cook and make things that store well days ahead, and whenever I have a minute to spare, I make cakes and store them for the vast number of visitors who come here. I make my own tea-time bread too, and I find homemade meringues can soften the hearts of many businessmen quicker than drinks! I think originally living in the Argentine with the only good shops over one hundred miles away taught me the secret of planning ahead, and of course nowadays life is made very easy by frozen and tinned foods. The thing is just to add your own ideas to these commodities to make them less conventional. We eat our meals in record time and have an awful job playing with our food if visitors come to a meal, they are so slow. It always seems dreadful that a meal which takes two hours to prepare can be eaten in under fifteen minutes and nothing is left to remember it by except a heap of washing up. Actually, I like washing up. I would not designate this chore to a machine for anything; it is almost a game to see how quickly it can be done. Unfortunately, my eyesight is not as good as it was. So maybe as age takes its toll and I get dimmer-sighted, I shall one day sink to having a dishwasher in self-defense.

My time is constantly interrupted by phone calls, curiously enough mostly at mealtimes, so with a quick swallow I try not to think of my food getting colder and colder as I listen sometimes to interminable stories of how good the dog is before the owner comes to the nitty-gritty of how bad it is and what should he or she do. They have seldom read my books or they would know the answer. Sometimes a brief time spent with

*No Bad Dogs,* borrowed from the library, has whetted their appetite to have a chat with me. I like people, and I like talking to people, but when you have anything up to three hundred letters a day, it is deadly. I have often begged people on television not to write to me with their problems, and soon I shall have to find some method of getting help as both my arms have become extremely painful with muscle cramp from too much typing and writing. The queries that come are all so different it is impossible to have stereotyped replies, and many are more concerned with human worries than canine ones. I get letters from as far away as Saudi Arabia, India, New Zealand and Australia. The stamps go to my grandchildren. I get invitations to go and stay in many parts of the world, including Bogotá, but I feel in these troubled days Croxley Green is probably the safest. I have no wish to be kidnapped in Bogotá, suffer an earthquake in Algeria or a typhoon in St Lucia, where I was not long before the last one.

As a result of my dog-training ventures and the successes of Juno and Junia, I often get asked to do demonstrations for charity, and have done literally hundreds over the years. I have also toured the United States and have shown on television and even in impromptu demonstrations in the street how dogs can be trained in a matter of minutes.

Lots of children write or phone me asking for advice on ponies. I do want to give advice to the growing number of animal-struck children there are around, many of whose parents phone me to ask how they should go about finding work in the stables for their girls. The chance of having a career with animals is very slim these days, so many people want to work with horses in riding stables. To all of them I say: by all means, do it. From the very beginning when you start earning money, put a little aside so that one day, if humanly possible, you can own an animal of your own. However much you enjoy working with horses, you will never get insight into a horse's mind working with other people's animals. But remember, owning a horse is a big responsibility. It cannot be left in a field without constant food or care. It might fall ill. And it is certainly not cheap to own a pony. Think hard before you make your decision.

# News and Views

How do I view the future at over seventy years of age?
Lots of people ask me what I am going to do now.
Well, I am not going to change. I am going to do
everything that is offered to me, and that I wish and
can physically do. I am going to take an enormous
interest in what goes on in the world. I think if I had
not taken up dog training and animal work I would
have liked to have been a lawyer. My mother always
said that I should have been a lawyer, because if there
is one thing I enjoy doing, it is having a really good
argument. That is why I like chat shows on the radio,
if I am given a bit of a challenge. I have always been
able to respond with quick repartee and I hope that as
long as my brain lasts and I do not get too senile, I can
continue in this way. I go on *Any Questions* sessions at
the local community center to keep my mind fresh and
I have done two *Any Questions* programs on radio.

One question that is put to me many times a day is, "What is it like to find yourself internationally famous at your age?" Well, I do not consider myself famous. I think that I have become well known through my public appearances and numerous articles and talks, but I would not call any of that famous. I do not think that dog trainers are really in a category to become famous. The famous people are those like Napoleon who have really done something in this world. I may have helped over seventeen thousand people to train their dogs and lead happier lives, but none of that constitutes fame.

It is, however, good fun to be well known. Wherever I go now I am recognized. I was in a butcher's shop recently when a little girl, not more than two years old, saw me through the window and called out, "Look Mummy, TV!" I was going down the escalator at Baker Street the other day and as a woman passed me going in the other direction she laughed and called out, "Walkies." When I got out at the station another voice called, "Sit," and when I gave my ticket up, the collector leaned across to his colleague and said, "She's on TV."

When I was mixing in the studios with people like Clark Gable, Gracie Fields, Alec Guinness and many more as a dog film star's trainer, I collected two volumes of autographs for my daughter, who was recovering from a serious illness. We look through these books sometimes and it helps to bring back some very happy and interesting memories.

One advantage is that I do get a certain amount of perks from being well known. I went into a shop the other day and bought a dress. I handed my bank card to the assistant as you have to do these days and she gave it back to me exclaiming, "Oh no, I don't want that. You are famous." I hope my credit will always be as good as that. Whatever I do now, I find everyone is much more helpful. I wanted to talk to a features editor on a major paper the other day, and asked the secretary to put me through. I heard her say, "Please sir, Barbara Woodhouse—*Walkies*—is on the telephone."

The fame that I have been favoured with will not alter our lives at all. I am unlikely even to get an extra holiday as my work has increased so much, with letters and telephone calls as well as my publishing business, which I run entirely on my own with my husband's help. I could not get away without being inundated with work on my return. I have no secretary and have little time to myself. I cannot understand why people strive and strive to have a lot of money. Money over a certain amount brings little pleasure. If one has the basic things in life with a little to spare for your near friends and family, that is fine. Personally, I have no wish to get myself a lot of extra things. I do not buy many clothes. I do not go often to a hairdresser and can do most things myself, so what good would a lot of money be to me?

When we moved to Campions we had to work very hard to get enough money to keep it up and to buy new land. It was the dogs' earnings which paid to have cowsheds built to my specifications with their film and television fees, but we pinched and scraped in those days to keep the place going and educate our three children properly. Things were a little easier when I began to earn more, and Michael too, of course, became a consultant, not just a G.P. We had no financial backing. That is why it was so risky when I made films. Often they cost little more than two hundred and fifty pounds but it was almost more than we could afford.

Even if we had a lot of money today, we would not know what to do with it. Anyway, there is no fun in earning a lot these days as the income tax is so high and you are not allowed to give it to your children. At one time we could have given the surplus of the amount we earned to our children, but with new tax laws we are only allowed to give them about three thousand pounds a year, so what good is earning? Much better to have a bit of peace.

Ingenuity has always enabled me to make money easily with new schemes, though not all of them work of course. Many years ago I had the good idea of making washable coloured nylon dog leads and collars, long before anyone else had thought of it. With the help of a very old business friend of mine, I had the nylon specially dyed for me in Manchester. My maid made five hundred leads and collars a day on our old Singer sewing machine. My husband used to stamp out the holes in the collars with a special eyelet machine and I used to wrap them in pairs and sizes and dispatch them all over England. Then a firm caught on to the idea and as I could not get a patent, I was out. Now every show dog today wears one of these collars and leads, and I can do nothing about it.

Another idea I hoped would make money was to write phrase books in foreign languages that gave all the household phrases instead of the ones usually listed. I sent my idea to several publishers who all turned it down so I decided to publish them myself. All went well except for the problem of the cover. The board cover I was recommended faded almost instantly and I had to pay the extra cost of getting dust covers made. Later we used laminated covers, but they were not so much in use then. I sold thirty-five thousand copies.

I am old-fashioned. I think the code by which one's parents brings one up stays with one for the rest of one's life. Those who deliberately defy that code are not the happiest of people. My mother spent endless hours teaching us things which when we were young seemed tedious, but we always paid attention, and now in later life I wish some of the youngsters today would be taught the same things.

Here are just a few of the lessons we learned.

One was never to overstay our welcome when we were invited out; for example, never stay longer than six o'clock when invited out to tea, and any hint, however slight, by a hostess, should be taken. Three other things which we were taught, and which I still think vital, were always to thank for a present immediately, never to be late for an appointment and always to answer letters promptly. Nowadays no one answers letters for weeks, nearly everyone is late for appointments and some of the youngsters do not ever bother to thank you for a present. If a thank-you letter arrives six weeks after the gift has been received, the giver, if it is me, feels aggrieved. I, in my busy life, have bothered to remember that gift, and given time to buy it and send it, so surely the recipient can take the trouble to give up five minutes to say thank you. I always say, just a postcard of acknowledgement is all I want. Being late for an appointment is a crime in my opinion. How can one plan a day's work if those you are supposed to meet are late? I feel so bad-tempered if anyone keeps me waiting that I do not want to see them. I remember the editor of a magazine once made an appointment to see me and he arrived one and a half hours late. I was so angry that in spite of the fact that I needed the publicity, I told him I could not see him and that he must make another appointment and keep it. I thought I would never see him again, but I did, and after that he was always punctual. Nowadays it is positively déclassé to be punctual, and people seem very surprised if one is. I remember telling a psychiatrist in conversation one day that my children always phoned me if they were going to be a few minutes later than they had said. He looked at me as if to say I should be ready to enter a mental home at any minute, and asked, "You do not mean the whole family is punctual, do you?" and when I said yes, I could see he thought me a future case for his notebook! I feel it is dishonest to be late; you are stealing someone's time—it does not matter whether it is your firm's time or just a private person's time. To many people, time is still money, yet those who offend would probably never think of stealing goods or money.

One other thing I shall always remember Mother telling us was to look people straight in the face when speaking to them. "The eyes are the mirror of one's soul," and if one has nothing to hide, then let people look into that mirror. In later years I have found this extremely useful when I trained dogs. Few dogs will attack you if you look them straight in the face. All dogs sense your love for them if you are looking at them with love, and most dogs sense that they have done wrong when you look at them with disgust. The expression in the eyes is the greatest help in animal training or making friends with animals, and I think it is the same with human beings. Eyes, I have often noticed, change colour when people are ill. The eyes of physically and mentally exhausted people go pale in colour and this happens with dogs too. A dog that is going to bite you shows the intention by its eyes changing colour. Few people notice this, but in my life I have had to, or I would have got bitten more times than I would have liked.

Lastly, Mother always told us to say sorry if we were in the wrong, and this is the thing I find hardest to do. To admit one is wrong is a personal loss of face, and I fear in my life I have often wriggled out of things when I have been in the wrong. The Irish call it "the gift of the gab," and I reckon that having been born in the Emerald Isle, I was given it by the little people at my christening. I have used it to tick people off until they have been insulted at every word, then I have twisted it around so that if they are on the telephone, they ask if they can come and see me, and if they do, we have become the best of friends. I have a sneaking feeling that some people enjoy a good ranting and raving, and like you for it, but my fault is that I seldom take back what I have said. It is a trait that I should try and conquer, but it is so easily got away with by the gift of the gab that I regret to say, even at my age, I still am often in the wrong without admitting it.

One of the things in modern days that I simply hate is bad language on the television and vulgar sex. I am sure if a play or talk was funny you would not need filth to make people laugh. Vulgarity in any form coarsens one. The old plays and films were good and funny and had nothing obscene. I now find myself listening to television plays in my drawing room where words I did not even know the meaning of until I was middle-aged are used. I feel that this country is going to—not the dogs for dogs are too nice—but possibly to some other more unpleasant animal such as snakes. We should pull our socks up before we sink too low. We do not have respect for ourselves. As my mother used to say in the old days: "If you use filthy language, it is not the person you are directing your talk to who gets hurt, it is you, and your soul that is forever damaged."

You must be courageous and rely on yourself. On the whole people are good. If they would give of themselves, of their work, of their best, I feel perfectly certain that this would be a happier world. Do not count on anyone else. I was persuaded once, when my writing and books began to be known, to get myself an agent. I did. He wrote to me to say that he was afraid there were no offers for my writings and that he could not do anything for me!

It is easy to overlook those who have had bad luck in their lives. I have always given special attention to handicapped people, helped them to train their dogs, as with the deaf, the armless and the blind.

Take a leaf out of their book. Never take no for an answer. Do not let people depress and cheat you, and smile and laugh as much as you possibly can.

Another piece of advice is never go to sleep with something undone. If you have inspiration, you must use it at once or something will stop you doing so. Luckily, I write as quickly as I read, but whether other people can read my writing I do not know! As I write, there is a film and television project afoot which will use ponies. I so want to do it, as I am always associated with dogs, whereas I have spent thirty years with horses, having in my girlhood broken in hundreds of horses in the Argentine, run a riding school, bought and sold horses and owned ponies. I told the publishers that I would only write the *Barbara Woodhouse Book of Dogs* if I could also write the *Barbara Woodhouse Book of Ponies*. As it turned out the dog book sold only a small amount and the pony book sold eighty thousand copies!

What worries me most in business today is that some people seem not to care about breaking their word. If I say I will do something or give a price for anything, I stick to it and would rather lose on the deal than go back on my word. But dozens of times in my life I have been let down flagrantly and I still will not learn. I get little sympathy for my mistakes in trusting people. "Oh, that's business, dear" is all I am told. Why should business be built very often, as far as I can gather, on deceit and lies?

Yet I have met a few absolutely wonderful people in the film business; one in particular, a quite small film distributor who for seventeen years made money for me and got every possible release for films I made on sixteen millimeters and had blown up to thirty-five millimeters for the cinema. When I met Eric Romer, known in the film world as Sax as he ran Saxon Films, he told me, "I will do my damnedest to get your films released because I like your enterprise. I have to take fifty percent of the earnings because I have to work very hard for what I get. If you can find someone else to get the films a showing at a lesser percentage, I do not mind in the least." It was worth every penny he took, not only because of the business he got for my films, but because he is without a doubt one of the nicest, kindest businessmen I have ever met. His advice was invaluable, his loyalty and sympathy to all my letdowns were perennial. Money cannot buy these qualities; they are inborn. I have never met anyone else in my whole life who gave me quite such a helping hand in show business so freely. It is a business where you come across hardheaded men whom you have to meet on equal terms. I loved making films but the fact that you are a small producer trying to get into a big man's world does not matter. Producers are not interested in giving a film a tryout to see what the public wants, and in my opinion, today they are stuffing filth down the audiences' throats ad nauseam. I am absolutely sure that audiences would love something clean and nice for a change from sex and murder.

There is still one thing I wish to achieve in my life, and that is to be able to slip immediately into conversation in as many languages as possible. My mother spoke six fluently, including Russian. I shall never achieve all this, but to me this is education, and until I can do something like this, I consider I am ill-educated, something I do not accept easily. Otherwise I think I have completed everything I have wanted to do.